Lesson Planning

Lesson planning is an essential component of every teacher's practice. It is part of a three-tiered, integrated pedagogy: planning, teaching and evaluation. Drawing on the work of skilful teachers and the latest research, this book provides a rationale for lesson planning as an integral part of a teacher's work. It introduces the key concepts and skills of lesson planning and provides a practical framework for their development.

This book helps the reader to make an informed choice about the approaches they use to plan lessons, taking into account their subject area and the requirements of individual learners. Covering all aspects of short-, medium- and long-term planning, chapters include:

- writing appropriate learning objectives and outcomes

- designing and structuring engaging teaching activities

- resourcing the lesson

- assessing students' learning

- strategies for personalised learning

- evaluating your lesson.

The book also includes a wide range of practical and reflective activities to help the reader apply the ideas discussed to their own work and key questions at the end of each chapter to encourage the development of their skilful pedagogy. This highly practical book is essential reading for trainee and practising teachers.

Jonathan Savage is a Reader in Education and Enterprise Fellow at the Institute of Education, Manchester Metropolitan University, UK. He teaches on various PGCE courses and doctoral studies programmes. Jonathan is also Managing Director of UCan Play, a not-for-profit company dedicated to supporting innovative approaches to education with technology.

Lesson Planning

Key concepts and skills for teachers

Jonathan Savage

Routledge
Taylor & Francis Group

LONDON AND NEW YORK

First published 2015
by Routledge
2 Park Square, Milton Park, Abingdon, Oxon OX14 4RN

and by Routledge
711 Third Avenue, New York, NY 10017

Routledge is an imprint of the Taylor & Francis Group, an informa business

© 2015 Jonathan Savage

The right of Jonathan Savage to be identified as author of this work has been asserted by him in accordance with sections 77 and 78 of the Copyright, Designs and Patents Act 1988.

British Library Cataloguing in Publication Data
A catalogue record for this book is available from the British Library

Library of Congress Cataloging in Publication Data
Savage, Jonathan.
  Lesson planning : key concepts and skills for teachers / Jonathan Savage.
    pages cm
  Includes bibliographical references and index.
  1. Lesson planning. I. Title.
  LB1027.4.S34 2014
  371.3028—dc23   2014002341

ISBN: 978–0–415–70895–1 (hbk)
ISBN: 978–0–415–70896–8 (pbk)
ISBN: 978–1–315–76518–1 (ebk)

Typeset in Melior
by Keystroke, Station Road, Codsall, Wolverhampton

Contents

Introduction

Welcome to this book on lesson planning! I hope you find it an informative and useful read. Lesson planning can be an enjoyable process that forms the bedrock of effective teaching in any classroom. Although much of this planning process should be done prior to the actual lesson being delivered, I will argue throughout this book that lesson planning is just one part of a three-tiered process of work that you will need to engage with in order to become a skilful teacher. It is intrinsically linked to other key activities such as the actual act of teaching itself and your ability to reflect on and evaluate your work. Together, these three interrelated cognitive and practical activities form a core part of what I am going to call your 'pedagogy'.

Lesson planning itself is a highly creative activity. It is underpinned by certain skills that you will need to develop. I have sequenced these skills throughout the main chapters of this book. For this reason, I would encourage you to read this book in a linear way and avoid the temptation to miss out chapters. In particular, I can anticipate that you might be keen to find out more about the lesson planning template that I am going to recommend you use. You will have to wait until Chapter 7 to find that (but please do not turn there now). I have deliberately put the documentation chapter towards the end of the book because there are so many other vital things that you need to think about before you get preoccupied with form-filling!

Done rigorously and conscientiously, lesson planning will challenge your thinking about your subject(s) and how you are going to teach effectively. Throughout this book, I have included a number of practical and reflective tasks for you to undertake. These activities are designed to help you think through the key issues that we will be considering and make links to your own teaching practice. If you are just starting out in teaching, perhaps by studying for a PGCE or working within a school-centred programme of initial teacher education, I hope that these activities will assist you in developing your teaching practice at this formative stage. If you are a more experienced teacher, I hope that these activities will help you reconsider the established ways of thinking and acting that your pedagogy already contains. Clearly, whether or not you do the activities is entirely up to you, but they all come from exercises and techniques that I have asked my own students to do over the years.

- What are the effective planning skills that a teacher needs?
- How will the skills of planning relate to the physical act of teaching and the process of reflecting on and evaluating that act?

Some basic questions

What are the big questions about lesson planning that we need to explore right at the beginning of this book? These are the ten most frequent questions I get asked:

- What is 'lesson planning'?

- What does a lesson plan contain?

- Does lesson planning always result in a written document, that is, a lesson plan?

- Do all my lessons have to be planned in the same way?

- Should my lesson plans look like those completed by other teachers?

- If two teachers are teaching the same class the same lesson, will their plans be identical?

- What about if I am teaching the same lesson to four different Year 7 classes? Can I use the same lesson plan each time?

- Is lesson planning something I have to do for my whole teaching career?

- Does a lesson plan have to have timings in it?

- Does a lesson have to be written on a particular lesson plan template?

I suspect that these are some of the basic questions that you may be asking. All these questions are entirely legitimate ones to ask but they do not have simple answers. Before you read on, why don't you ask yourself how you would answer these ten questions.

The purpose of this introductory chapter is twofold: first, to explore some of the above questions and provide some basic initial responses to them; second, to introduce the main content of this book which will explore these and other questions in greater detail.

So, here we go. Let's cut to the chase and try to address some of these basic and most frequently asked questions about lesson planning head on.

Q1: What is 'lesson planning'?

Lesson planning, for me, is 'the process of thinking through and writing down a plan for the teaching of, and learning within, a lesson that I will be teaching to a specific group of students in a specific place at a specific time'.

This is my standard definition for lesson planning. It means that my lesson plans will not be the same year by year. Why? Because the students I am teaching will change, as may the space I am working within, or the time that I am teaching them at. So, can you do lesson planning in your head? Is the writing down optional? No! For me, it is important that there is a written document. Why? See questions 2 and 3 below.

Q2: What does a lesson plan contain?

A lesson plan is a written document that outlines the key features of the sequence of teaching that will result in you teaching something and your students learning something. It needs to have the following elements as a minimum: learning objectives, learning outcomes, teaching activities, resources, a differentiation strategy and an assessment strategy. Is that it? No, but these are the essential elements in my view.

Q3: Does lesson planning always result in a written document, that is, a lesson plan?

Yes. The process of writing the lesson plan is an integral part of its formal development. The process of writing something down takes an idea out of your head and externalises it in a new way and in a new form. It allows you to perceive it differently and situate it alongside other ideas in ways that are difficult to achieve through mental juggling. By the way, I do not fully understand how this works but know that it does and my basic understanding of our neurology tells me that this is the case.

Q4: Do all my lessons have to be planned in the same way?

No. There are numerous ways that you can plan lessons. However, experience has taught me that there is a good way to start students in their engagement with lesson planning and this is what is outlined in this book. At a certain point (and this varies from person to person), you will begin to forge your own way ahead on the bedrock of skills and approaches that you have explored here. I am sure that over time you will become much more proficient than I am at planning fantastic and engaging lessons.

Q5: Should my lesson plans look like those completed by other teachers?

Maybe, at least to start with. But, as I said in my response to question 4, you will find your own approach in this process and at that point you only need to justify your planning approach to yourself (and perhaps to your headteacher or Ofsted on occasions too!).

Q6: If two teachers are teaching the same class the same lesson, will their plans be identical?

No. A good rule of thumb is never to teach a lesson using someone else's lesson plan. Why? Your own identity as a teacher is too important to sacrifice on the altar of someone else's planning. Isn't that a bit dramatic? No, I don't think it is. Read the rest of this book to find out why.

Q7: What about if I am teaching the same lesson to four different Year 7 classes? Can I use the same lesson plan each time?

No. Revise the answer to question 1 and look at my key definition again. Just like your own identity as a teacher, this is too important to be taken for granted (see question 6); your students as individuals and as a class are too important to be lumped together and treated the same. Every class you teach will be different. You must plan for their individual needs and requirements if you want to become a brilliant teacher.

Q8: Is lesson planning something I have to do for my whole teaching career?

Yes and no. I suspect that at a certain point in your career the lesson planning process will become almost second nature. It will become a mental process that you will still engage with but by then it is probably ok to stop writing so much stuff down. Until then, refer to my answer to question 3.

Q9: Does a lesson plan have to have timings in it?

Timings are helpful to assist you in planning for a good and steady flow in a lesson. The process of planning the times for particular steps of the lesson, and then teaching that lesson in light of that plan, will help you develop a perception for the flow of learning that you will not get if you do not think about the timings of teaching activities. So, short answer, yes!

Q10: Does a lesson have to be written on a particular lesson plan template?

No. There is no golden template that you must use. I am going to introduce a couple of examples in Chapter 7. But before then, we have some important groundwork to do first. So no sneaky looking ahead!

PRACTICAL TASK

Review the answers to the ten questions above. Were any of the answers surprising? When you get the opportunity, sit down with an experienced teacher and ask them the same ten questions. Compare and contrast their answers with yours and mine.

The structure of this book

Following this introduction, this book is structured in eight chapters. As I have mentioned already, please avoid the temptation to dip in and out of the chapters. They have been written in sequence and with a sense of structuring the cognitive and conceptual work you need to undertake to plan for effective teaching and learning in mind.

Chapter 2 begins this process by focusing on learning objectives and learning outcomes. Establishing clear learning objectives and outcomes is an essential part of effective lesson planning. This chapter will introduce the key skills needed to make informed choices about learning objectives and outcomes, as well as sequence these appropriately across lessons. It will target 'learning', rather than 'activities', and show how it is vital that you think clearly about the key learning that you want to include within your lesson. Teaching activities will not be the primary focus at this stage. The chapter will conclude with a presentation of a simple approach designed to help you construct learning outcomes in a three-tiered way. This will be explored in more detail in Chapter 6.

Following the formation of appropriate learning objectives and outcomes, Chapter 3 will explore the next stage of the lesson planning process: the design of engaging teaching activities. These activities will be drawn from a range of sources. However, it is your responsibility to structure them in an appropriate way for your lesson. The key test here is to focus the teaching activities in such a way as to engage students and facilitate the key learning objectives and outcomes that have been identified. This chapter will examine a range of common types of activities, drawn from numerous subject areas and phases of education. It will also show how key elements such as student curiosity and motivation can be fostered through the design of these teaching activities. Finally, the chapter will examine how teaching activities can be structured within the lesson.

Teaching does not take place in a vacuum. The resources that you choose and use have a major part to play in facilitating effective teaching and learning. Chapter 4 will explore a framework for the analysis and evaluation of common resources that you might use and will promote the idea that students' interest can be captured by the uses of unfamiliar objects too. Ultimately, as with every area of lesson planning, you will need to make informed choices about the resources you use within your teaching. Being able to justify these choices pedagogically is a key skill.

Having a strategy for assessing students' learning is an integral part of the lesson plan. Whilst broad strategies for summative assessment (e.g. end of unit assessments) have their place, Chapter 5 will emphasise the importance of what has commonly been referred to as 'assessment for learning' techniques. This chapter will introduce a range of these techniques. As with every element of lesson planning, informed choices that can be justified to others are better than uninformed choices made in an arbitrary fashion. Therefore, in this chapter I will be emphasising how the strategies chosen to assess students' learning in an individual lesson need to be related closely to the learning objectives and outcomes that have been established earlier in the lesson plan. I will also consider how you can build a positive environment for assessment in your classroom before concluding the chapter with a strong argument for assessment being embedded within the core activities of planning, teaching and reflection.

However students are grouped within the school, it is my strong belief that any teacher who is teaching more than one student at a time is teaching a mixed-ability class. Personalisation, and the closely related pedagogical strategy of differentiation, should be key elements of every lesson plan. The individual needs of specific students, or groups of students, will not be met by accident. As with assessment, teachers need to make deliberate choices about specific techniques to ensure that every student within their class has the opportunity to learn in the most effective way. Chapter 6 will introduce a broad range of strategies that are commonly used to help personalise learning and provide an evaluative framework to help you make informed choices for your own lesson plan.

Up to this point in the book, no specific lesson plan documentation has been introduced. The previous chapters (Chapter 2–6) have covered the key elements of lesson planning and these will now be considered in light of the lesson plan document itself. In Chapter 7 two lesson plan documents will be presented, with the pros and cons of each being discussed. Rather than insisting on you having to adopt a particular approach, I will encourage you to make an informed choice about your lesson plan template in light of the specific subject or topic you are teaching (and in acknowledgement of your own school or university/training provider's requirements). I will also discuss how the individual lesson plan itself relates to broader processes of medium- and longer-term curriculum planning (such as 'unit of work' and 'curriculum overview map' documentation).

Chapter 8 is a really important chapter. Within it, I will explore how the lesson plan document itself structures the 'performance' of teaching. To do this, I will draw on a number of metaphors that demonstrate how the lesson plan document can helpfully inform the actions of the teacher, minute-by-minute, throughout the lesson. Lesson planning, as a cognitive and conceptual activity, has to be considered in close relationship to the actual events and actions that will take place in your classroom. This chapter will explore how this can be done.

Similarly, once the 'performance' of the lesson has been delivered, the evaluation of the lesson needs to be undertaken. This is the vital third component of an effective pedagogy. Chapter 9 will draw together the book's main themes and help you to develop a constructive approach to lesson evaluation that views the lesson plan itself and the 'performance' of the lesson as two sides of the same coin. Key links will be made between aspects of educational evaluation and the abilities needed to be a reflective practitioner. I will conclude the chapter with some wider points about a constructive approach to your continuing professional development.

I trust that you will find this book a valuable tool in learning to plan engaging and exciting lessons for your students. Please let me know how you get on!

2 Writing appropriate learning objectives and outcomes

Introduction

Establishing clear learning objectives and outcomes is an essential part of effective lesson planning. In this chapter I will introduce the key skills needed to make informed choices about learning objectives and outcomes, as well as considering how you can sequence these appropriately across lessons. I will target 'learning', rather than 'activities', and show how it is vital to think clearly about the key learning that you want to include within your lessons. Teaching activities in and of themselves will not be the primary focus within this chapter (we will come on to this in Chapter 3). This chapter will conclude with a presentation of a simple approach designed to help you 'stage' learning outcomes in a three-tiered way. This will be explored in more detail in Chapter 6 when we turn our attention to the related issues of personalisation and differentiation.

REFLECTIVE TASK

The lessons that you prepare and teach to your students do not take place in a vacuum. Before we turn our attention to the learning objectives and outcomes that you will want to design for a specific lesson that you are teaching, right at the beginning of this book it is a good time to reflect for a moment or two about the key aims of your teaching. Ask yourself the following key questions:

- Why have I come into teaching?
- What am I hoping that my teaching will achieve?
- How does my teaching relate to the key aims of the institution that I am working within?

The broad aims of education

In my day-to-day life, I work on a number of different courses of initial teacher education including preparing primary school teachers through an undergraduate degree programme that leads to qualified teacher status, as well as working with postgraduate students on a Postgraduate Certificate in Education course. Interviewing students for these courses takes up a good part of every year but it is always a fascinating process. Potential students give many reasons for wanting to become a teacher. But perhaps some of the most common reasons that I hear (and I think that this is because these are the most important) are that students are wanting to contribute something to the education of the next generation, to give something back to others, to help inspire others to love the things that they have loved and to help young people to make a difference in their lives. These charitable aims or ambitions are praiseworthy and something that all teachers should take a moment to reflect on. In the hurly-burly of school life, it is often difficult to find the time or space to reflect on the key purposes behind all the activity that we do as teachers. But to do so is important. Through this, we can help maintain a healthy and positive attitude towards our work and our students.

Additionally, this kind of reflective activity can help us in our dealings with students. How many times have you been asked 'Why are we doing this?' in a lesson that you have taught? Sometimes that question can be asked out of boredom; sometimes it is asked out a sense of genuine enquiry and needs a productive answer.

Broad educational aims of the type that underpin our work in schools are expressed in a range of places, normally in eloquent language that can seem a bit imposing. The National Curriculum is one place where these aims have been expressed in various ways. In the previous version of the National Curriculum (DCSF 2008), the following statement appeared which emphasised the important link between school and society:

> Education influences and reflects the values of society, and the kind of society we want to be. It is important, therefore, to recognise a broad set of common values, aims and purposes that underpin the school curriculum and the work of schools.

> Clear aims that focus on the qualities and skills learners need to succeed in school and beyond should be the starting point for the curriculum. These aims should inform all aspects of curriculum planning and teaching and learning at whole-school and subject levels.

> The curriculum should enable all young people to become:

> - Successful learners who enjoy learning, make progress and achieve

> - Confident individuals who are able to live safe, healthy and fulfilling lives

> - Responsible citizens who make a positive contribution to society. (ibid., p. 4)

This statement sets the National Curriculum in a national context. It encourages us to think about education as being linked to the values of our society in a fundamental and symbiotic way. The education of children, it suggests, influences the values of our society; the values of our society inform the educational aims and purposes of the curriculum and the work of schools. In this model, the National Curriculum and the work of schools are intertwined.

Into this mix, the development of young people is considered. The specific role of the National Curriculum, as interpreted by schools and delivered to young people, is to produce successful learners, confident individuals and responsible citizens.

Personally, I like the sentiments expressed within these words. However, the National Curriculum being delivered from September 2014 is significantly shorter. In the overall framework document that has been published, sections 3.1 and 3.2 express the aims of the National Curriculum as follows:

> 3.1 The national curriculum provides pupils with an introduction to the essential knowledge they need to be educated citizens. It introduces pupils to the best that has been thought and said, and helps engender an appreciation of human creativity and achievement.
>
> 3.2 The national curriculum is just one element in the education of every child. There is time and space in the school day and in each week, term and year to range beyond the national curriculum specifications. The national curriculum provides an outline of core knowledge around which teachers can develop exciting and stimulating lessons to promote the development of pupils' knowledge, understanding and skills as part of the wider school curriculum. (DfE 2013)

In this language, the curriculum is explicitly linked to knowledge. Thankfully, schools are able to contextualise the National Curriculum, alongside other frameworks for the management of teaching and learning, in their own way. Aspirational language about the broad aims and purposes of education can be found on many school websites. Here is one example from the school where both my sons have been educated:

> The core values of Sandbach School are those embodied in the School's motto and crest displayed on all uniform badges and school documentation. Such values are known, understood and should be practised by all members of the Sandbach School Community.
>
> The Latin motto 'Ut Severis Seges' broadly translates as 'As you sow, so shall you reap' or the more you put into school life, the more you will get out of it. The crest of the Cheshire wheatsheaf suggests that care, nurturing and commitment are needed to achieve a harvest of quality. Applying both concepts to an all-boys comprehensive school, the values which the motto and crest encapsulate are:
>
> ■ Commitment to excellence in all aspects of school life – working hard and playing hard;

- Respect for self and others, combined with a responsibility and caring for all members of the school and its wider community;

- Integrity, honesty and openness in how every member of the school community operates;

- Encouragement of all to be creative, innovative and able to take initiative in order to develop every individual beyond their perceived potential. (Sandbach School 2012)

This statement from Sandbach School identifies and defines these core values for members of the school community before extending these into the wider community within which the school is situated. Having spent many hours at the school, whether it be for a parents' evening, rugby match or music concert, I can attest to the fact that these values do make a day-to-day difference in the life of the school. It is not uncommon to hear teachers refer to them in conversation with the boys, or to see them picked up in letters to parents from the headteacher, or to see them displayed on the walls as a reminder to students (and teachers) that their community has been established on certain key principles.

I believe that these kinds of statements are important. They set a tone for the work of a school and provide a reference or frame for our work as individual teachers within it. Although it is less common to find such statements about the aims and values of education from individual teachers, having a broader set of aims for our work with young people is important at an individual level. Spending time thinking hard about why we are investing our time and energy into the teaching of our young people is something that all teachers should do regularly.

In our discussion so far, we have considered how the broad aims of national educational frameworks such as the National Curriculum and decisions made by schools about their core values are important contexts for both your lesson planning and the decisions you will make within those plans for specific learning objectives and outcomes. But before we turn our attention to those specific elements, there is a third vitally important context that we need to consider.

The importance of the subject

For many teachers, the love of a particular subject is a key motivating factor for becoming a teacher. The opportunity to develop one's subject and teach others about it is high up the list of most teachers' job satisfaction (Spear et al. 2000, p. 52). We also know that subject knowledge (by which I mean the actual knowledge of the subject but also, implicitly, the way that the subject is presented and traditionally taught) is a strong, formative force on the work of young teachers. But a preoccupation with a subject needs to be understood in a wider sense as you begin to think about planning sequences of learning for your students. Subjects, like the curriculum itself, are located within a context within which various collisions take place!

School subjects provide a context where antecedent structures collide with contemporary action; the school subject provides an obvious manifestation of historical legacies with which contemporary actors have to work. (Goodson 1991, p. 118)

Have you ever asked yourself why school communities are normally entirely organised around subject boundaries? Despite many attempts to do otherwise, whether in primary or secondary education, subjects have been the default organising construct (in terms of timetabling, lessons, resources and staffing) for many years. The quotation from Goodson provides us with an important link from society, within which the school is located, and the concept of individual subjects that the school provides sequences of instruction within. My view is that subjects provide a broad categorisation for understanding the world; they help us perceive and organise what could be seen as an overwhelming amount of knowledge in a focused way; they also provide a helpful framework by which the skills, processes and understanding we need to understand the world can be developed. Whilst all these things could be considered as beneficial, it is important to also remember that subjects do divide and compartmentalise knowledge and understanding in unhelpful ways too.

As Goodson notes, as a teacher within a school you will work in a primarily subject-based culture. His argument is that these subjects contain pre-existing structures, or ways of thinking, that may challenge the ways in which you and your students think today. In other words, subjects are underpinned by significant and powerful historical legacies. The potential for tension here can lead to fundamental differences of opinion about what should be taught within a particular subject, how it should be taught and how it should be assessed. For example, Jephcote and Davies give a flavour of the complexity of the situation by picking up on Goodson's notion of the 'teacher as actor' – someone who has to work within at least three different contexts or levels in order to present the subject as a meaningful 'whole' within the curriculum:

Changing the curriculum is an outcome of contexts between actors in different arenas and at different levels. Its story needs to be told at a number of levels to reflect the membership and structure of subject communities and to provide a means of illustrating each level and their interconnectedness. At the micro-level accounts have been concerned mainly with teachers, school classrooms and subjects and at macro-level with processes of policy-making and its implementation. At the same time, the meso-level has been taken to comprise of subject associations, local education authorities and sponsored curriculum projects where there are mediating processes which provide means to reinterpret macro-level changes and to assess the range of new choices they present to subject factions. (Jephcote and Davies 2007, p. 208)

Subjects, they argue, have a range of competing values, definitions and interests (ibid., p. 210) that can lead to conflict and tension, both within and across subjects

(Cooper 1983, p. 208). Goodson and Mangen's concept of a 'subject culture' is highly instructive here. Subject cultures are, they argue, the 'identifiable structures which are visibly expressed through classroom organisation and pedagogical styles' (Goodson and Mangen 1998, p. 120). They are what makes a particular subject unique and, in a simple sense, they are what portrays to students the sense that they are studying a particular subject at a specific moment in the school day.

Whether it is within the primary school or the secondary school, the idea that curriculum subjects are harmonious and homogeneous in their relationships with one another is false. As we begin the move towards planning your own individual lessons, it is vital to understand that an individual subject's 'subjectivities' are powerful influences on your way of thinking and acting within that subject. For primary school teachers, you will have noticed that there are many different ways of thinking about, and acting within, the various subjects that you are required to teach. A key component of any programme of initial teacher education in this phase introduces students not only to the key knowledge within a specific subject but also the key ways of thinking and acting within it. In my own teaching, I try to instil in my students a number of key ways of thinking and acting in music – for example, teach music by doing music; if you can say it, you can play it; use musical games whenever possible to teach musical processes. The same will be true in all the other subject areas that you have to cover.

Within secondary school initial teacher education, perhaps subjects play an even more significant role. Much larger chunks of time are spent in subject specialist groups where the ethos of a particular subject culture is cultivated and developed. However, any good programme of initial teacher education at this phase will also facilitate an interdisciplinary approach to students' understanding of their own and others' subject cultures. This might be through the examination of particular themes within a programme of professional issues; more imaginatively, it might be through students from one subject working with another group to share specific pedagogical aspects of their subject cultures. An obvious example of this from my own university has been when students studying for a PGCE in Drama have shared their understanding of the importance of teachers 'performing' and using their voices effectively with students in other subject areas.

I am labouring the importance of the subject culture here for a specific reason. Whatever type of school you are working within, the subject dimension of lesson planning is probably going to be at the forefront of your mind. It will be the starting point for your lesson planning process. It is vital that you seek to understand the formative ideas within a subject culture and that you are able to interrogate these in a constructive way.

As an example of this, in the following case study, an art teacher explores the links between the National Curriculum, her subject – Art – and her views of how it should be taught. Please note that the references to the National Curriculum in this teacher's account of her work are to the previous (2008) Programme of Study:

As an art teacher, creativity is central to my work. I wouldn't be where I am today without it. Creativity is key to my own making practices. I try to utilise every opportunity to bring creative processes into my own teaching. The National Curriculum is helpful in this respect. At Key Stage 3, creativity is the first Key Concept for Art and Design. This is what it says:

> There are a number of key concepts that underpin the study of art, craft and design. Pupils need to understand these concepts in order to deepen and broaden their knowledge, skills and understanding.
>
> ### 1.1 Creativity
> a. Producing imaginative images, artefacts and other outcomes that are both original and of value;
> b. Exploring and experimenting with ideas, materials, tools and techniques;
> c. Taking risks and learning from mistakes.

I really like some of the verbs in this definition: exploring, experimenting, producing. I also like that it mentions taking risks and learning from mistakes. This is really important in all artists' working practices.

Recently, I wanted to find ways to collaborate with other colleagues in my school. We'd look together at some of the cross-curricular dimensions but this didn't seem to inspire us very much. On the QCDA website, I noticed that they had a tool for comparing subjects together side-by-side. This got me thinking. Which other subjects had creativity as a Key Concept?

I was surprised to find that most other subjects did! I quite liked the definition of creativity in the programme of study for English:

> a. Making fresh connections between ideas, experiences, texts and words, drawing on a rich experience of language and literature;
> b. Using inventive approaches to making meaning, taking risks, playing with language and using it to create new effects;
> c. Using imagination to convey themes, ideas and arguments, solve problems, and create settings, moods and characters;
> d. Using creative approaches to answering questions, solving problems and developing ideas.

This seemed to contain similar ideas to that found within the Art and Design programme of study. It seemed to be encouraging a playfulness in using language that fitted well within my own views and the way that I work as an artist.

The contextualisation of a subject, in this case 'Art', within the educational 'subject culture' is a strong formative influence on your work as a teacher. It goes beyond issues of knowledge or content, and fundamentally influences your pedagogy, the way in which you teach. In the first part of this chapter, I have focused on three important contexts or frames for your work: the broad aims of education as defined by important legislative frameworks such as the National Curriculum; the important values that schools choose to adopt and use to establish their sense of identity within a local community; and the important and powerful frameworks of individual subjects and their subject cultures. At the beginning of your teaching career, it is vital that you question these assumptions. As you begin to plan your lessons and set learning objectives and outcomes for your teaching, it is vital that you can contextualise these in your own mind as well as provide justifications for these to students, parents and other staff that you are responsible to.

REFLECTIVE TASK

Spend some time analysing your own thoughts about these three important contexts for your own work. How do you interpret the principles of the National Curriculum in relation to your own thoughts about your subject(s)? If you are based in a school, or about to visit one for a teaching placement, what can you find out about that school's core values or mission within its local community? What tensions are there within your own subject area(s) and how are they explored within the subject communities that you are part of?

All of the above contextual work is really important in locating your own thinking at this formative stage. But it is time for us to turn our attention to the first practical task in lesson planning: defining your learning objective(s) for a lesson.

Lesson planning stage one: defining your learning objective(s)

Learning objectives are the most important part of your lesson plan. It is absolutely vital that you understand what is meant by a learning objective and how it is used as a foundation upon which all the other elements of the lesson plan are structured. We will consider learning objectives through the use of some key questions.

I What should learning objectives focus on?

You might think that this is an obvious question. They should focus on learning. But, as will become apparent, I have found this to be one of the most commonly misunderstood questions in my experience as a teacher educator.

Learning objectives define the learning that you want the students to engage in throughout the lesson. At this point, there is a legitimate question to ask about whether or not it is possible to define, in advance of the lesson, the learning that students will actually engage in. It is true to say that students will learn many different things throughout a lesson. Some of these will be expected and planned for by yourself; others may be unexpected and come as a surprise. There are some really difficult philosophical and conceptual questions that one could ask at this point. However, we will leave those to one side for the moment (although they will be picked up on later in the book) and make the assumption that it is fairly safe to assume that it is possible to predict the learning that a forthcoming lesson may contain.

Learning objectives must focus on the learning that the lesson will contain. They must not focus on the activities of the lesson that the students are going to do. The following statements *are not* learning objectives:

- Students will conduct an experiment to test the pH value of a range of solutions.

- Students will run 100m in the quickest time possible.

- Students will evaluate a range of different perspectives and sources surrounding the tactical decisions made by Sir Francis Drake.

All these statements describe an activity of some sort – conducting an experiment in a science class, physical exertion in terms of a race, or cognitive activity in terms of reading and evaluating. But none of them tell us exactly what is being learnt by the student undertaking the activity. For this reason, these statements cannot be described as learning objectives.

PRACTICAL TASK

Consider each of the above statements again. How could they be turned from a statement that describes activity into a statement that describes learning? What kinds of things do you think that this science, PE and history teacher would want their students to learn by engaging in these activities?

The misunderstanding between a 'learning' objective and a 'doing' objective is one of the most common misunderstandings that I see in my work as a teacher educator. It is easier to describe what your students are going to do in any given lesson; it is harder to describe what they are going to learn by doing it. But this distinction is at the heart of writing a good learning objective.

In order to form quality learning objectives for your lesson plan, a good place to start is by considering the following three simple questions:

1 What do I want the class to learn?

2 Why do I want them to learn it?

3 What do I need to do to enable them to learn it?

Which of these questions relate directly to our discussion of learning objectives? The first two questions are the key ones here. Once you have been able to answer these questions, then you can move on to the third question and begin to think about the construction of teaching activities that will enable them to engage with and explore the learning objectives you have formulated. We will discuss this third question further in Chapter 3. I want to stress this point. Please do not start to consider question 3 until questions 1 and 2 have been addressed fully.

PRACTICAL TASK

Think about an actual, or imagined, lesson that you are going to teach in the next week or so. Work through the three questions above but be very strict with yourself about answering them in the correct order. Try to write one sentence for each question that sums up your thought process.

Recently, I observed a student teacher teaching a Year 7 class in a local secondary school. The teacher was teaching the class about choosing particular sounds for varying expressive purposes within the context of a unit of work on programme music (music that tells a story or sets up a scene in the listener's mind). For her, she might have answered these three questions in the following way:

1 What do I want the class to learn? *I want the class to learn that the choice of a sound has an important role to play in creating a certain mood or atmosphere in the mind of the listener.*

2 Why do I want them to learn it? *I want the class to learn this because in order to be an effective composer, you need to understand the skills involved in choosing and editing an individual sound for an expressive purpose.*

3 What do I need to do to enable them to learn it? *I want to play games with the students using various sounds that I have selected to create a whole class composition. After that, I want to ask them to work in pairs on their own short compositions to accompany a short film clip that I have chosen.*

Which of these questions would have been appropriate to turn into a learning objective for this music lesson? Well, not the answer to question 3. Instead, her learning objective might have read something like this:

Students will learn to choose and edit sounds for an expressive purpose.

Or, perhaps:

> *Students will develop their understanding of how individual sounds create*
> *certain moods or atmospheres in the minds of an audience.*

Or something along those lines.

In this section so far, I have emphasised the fundamental point that learning objectives need to be about the learning that you want students to engage in during the lesson. I have laboured this point and given examples of different approaches. I have suggested a simple way into this process through the use of three simple questions.

2 How long does a learning objective need to be?

Following on from the question about what a learning objective should focus on, the second question I want us to consider involves the length of the learning objective. I would encourage you to try to avoid the temptation to overcomplicate learning objectives. Keep them short and focused. Personally, I would try to keep them to around 20–25 words at a maximum. In my visits to various schools around the north west of England, I see a range of advice about this. One piece of advice that I like is to keep learning objectives SMART. In other words, keep them:

- **S**pecific

- **M**easurable

- **A**ttainable

- **R**elevant

- **T**imely

Please note that you do not have to describe how they are all these things in the actual learning objective itself. Otherwise they may end up being a couple of hundred words long! But these headings give you some helpful key points to consider as you are choosing and writing your learning objectives for a specific lesson. Keep your learning objectives concise.

PRACTICAL TASK

Consider your answers to the first two questions in the previous practical task (what do I want the class to learn and why do I want them to learn it). Try to turn your response to these questions into two different learning objectives, each one between 20 and 25 words in total. Keep in mind the requirement to keep your learning objectives SMART.

3 How many learning objectives should a lesson have?

Quite often I am asked by students how many learning objectives any one lesson ought to have. My normal answer is one or two. Why? Learning objectives need to be carefully defined. They need to relate to the learning that you anticipate that the students will engage in. They also need to be selective.

Before I can answer this question more fully, I need to return to a point that I made above when I discussed whether or not it was possible to define, in advance, what students might learn in any individual lesson. The simple answer is that it is possible, in general, to define these things. Teaching is not a random exercise in hopefulness! With experience comes knowledge about the common pathways of learning. Learning objectives can act as useful signposts upon that journey.

However, it is important to acknowledge that although students will learn many things in any one lesson that you teach, it is quite right for you to have a legitimate focus on one or two of these key areas of learning. But please note that this does not in any way diminish the importance of the other learning that occurs. The learning objectives that you set for one lesson will be followed by different learning objectives for the following lesson, and different ones for the lesson after that. They will become part of a sequence of learning.

If I want to drive to Oswestry from Sandbach, I know that along the way I will pass through various other towns (notably Crewe, Nantwich, Whitchurch and Ellesmere). These towns are intermediate but important landmarks in my journey to Oswestry. In exactly the same way, learning objectives for individual lessons can be contextualised within a unit of work that culminates in the students reaching a new destination in their learning journey. We will consider this further in Chapter 7 when we spend some time looking at different forms of documentation including a Curriculum Overview Map and Unit of Work framework.

So, to pursue this analogy a little further, whilst the main two towns in my journey are Sandbach and Oswestry, an acknowledgement of the other towns in between helps me understand the journey that I am undertaking. The other towns are there to help me get from Sandbach to Oswestry, but they are not my main focus. Similarly, your choice of learning objectives will be selective. They will preclude certain other elements of learning that a lesson may contain, but they will allow you to helpfully focus on the key aspects of learning that you have chosen to prioritise for that particular lesson. This type of selective prioritisation of learning objectives is part of your skilful pedagogy as a teacher.

For now, be confident that it is entirely within your remit as a teacher to set one or two carefully considered learning objectives for a lesson that you are teaching. The particular choices that you make here will have consequences for all other aspects of your lesson plan, including the design of the teaching activities which will serve as the method of engagement through which students will actively explore and engage with the learning objective you have chosen. We discuss this further in the next chapter. They will also fundamentally influence what resources you choose to use in your lesson (Chapter 4), what you choose to focus on as you assess your students' learning in the lesson (Chapter 5), and the way in which you personalise and differentiate the teaching activities within your lesson (of which more in Chapter 6). If you have too many learning objectives in one lesson, you will not be able to make these important links in any meaningful way and the main thrust of the lesson will be diluted in an unhelpful manner. In my experience, this normally happens when you have three or more learning objectives within any one lesson.

> **REFLECTIVE TASK**
>
> Consider the learning outcomes that you wrote in the previous practical task. What other learning might students engage with during a lesson that had those as the key learning objectives? To what extent are these intermediate learning objectives?

Enough questions! Our immediate concern in this chapter is how the learning objectives relate to the next vitally important element of the lesson plan: the learning outcomes.

Lesson planning stage two: defining your learning outcomes

Whilst learning objectives describe the learning that students will engage with and explore throughout a lesson, learning outcomes are statements that describe what students will be doing in your lesson to demonstrate that they have understood, appreciated and applied the learning objectives that you have set for that particular lesson.

Over the years I have noticed that many teachers describe their learning outcomes in various ways. One of the most common that I have noticed is the following:

- All students will . . .

- Most students will . . .

- Some students will . . .

This seems like a simple and helpful way to describe the learning outcomes that might flow from a specific learning objective. To do this though, you will need to think carefully about the sequencing of the responses that students will make to the learning objective. This requires you to understand the processes of development that underpin the learning associated with a particular activity.

I think that this can be done in at least two ways. First, you can sequence the learning outcomes by activity. Put simply, if all students can do X, then most students can do X + Y and some students can do X + Y + Z. Learning outcomes by accretion seem quite common.

However, there are other ways that this can be done. Learning outcomes could be about the quality of engagement with a specific aspect of learning. So, if all students can do X, then most students can do X even better and some students will be doing it even better than that. In this model, you will need to think about exactly what is meant by 'doing it better' in relation to the opening learning outcome.

In some ways, these two approaches are broadly similar and depend on the words that you use within your learning outcome statements. However, I think that as a starting point they are a useful pair of ideas for thinking about how learning outcomes might work. We will consider a couple of examples to illustrate these points.

Earlier in the chapter I suggested that the phrase 'students will run 100m in the quickest time possible' was not a very good learning objective because it describes an activity rather than the learning that might be contained within an activity. Through a practical task, I asked you to consider what a more suitable learning objective might be for this. Clearly, without knowing the context of the lesson it is hard to be definitive. But, for sake of argument, a better learning objective for this might be: students will learn to position themselves in the starting blocks and adopt a relaxed disposition in preparation for the 100m sprint.

What would the learning outcomes for this learning objective be? Following the first model above, they might read something like this:

- All students will position themselves in a positive position in order to achieve a good, explosive start to their 100m sprint.

- Most students will position themselves in a positive position and show evidence of a relaxed disposition prior to the commencement of the 100m sprint.

- Some students will position themselves in a positive position and show evidence of a relaxed disposition, resulting in a significant improvement to their start times in the 100m sprint.

You can probably tell from this that I am not a PE teacher, but I hope that the point is clear. In the first 'version' of a set of learning outcomes, I am differentiating learning outcomes by adding content to each one.

Moving back to familiar ground, what would a set of learning outcomes following the second approach read like? Let us reconsider the example from the music lesson explored above, where the stated learning objective of the young music teacher might have been: students will learn to choose and edit sounds for an expressive purpose.

Following this second approach, her learning outcomes might have read as follows:

- All students will be able to choose and edit sounds for an expressive purpose and be able to justify their choice to a fellow member of the class.

- Most students will be able to do the above and give a fuller justification of how such sounds might be perceived by others in a specific compositional context.

- Some students will be able to do the above and develop a detailed analysis of how individual sounds might be perceived in different ways according to presentation and context within an individual compositional context.

In some ways, of course, this has similarities to the first approach in that the learning outcomes are becoming gradually more complex. However, in this second example I would argue that the complexity is primarily around the specific learning objective and the students' engagement with that specifically. It is not primarily about adding in alternative dimensions of learning that might signify a broader or more sophisticated understanding.

In the context of your lesson planning, these distinctions may not be that important to start with. However, I do think it is important to understand that there is more than one way to frame your learning outcomes. But the key point here is that learning outcomes, however they are expressed and organised, will give you key behaviours, attitudes or approaches to learning that you will be able to see as your students work throughout the lesson.

PRACTICAL TASK

Take one of the learning objectives that you defined in the early practical tasks and write two sets of learning objectives using the three-tiered approach outlined above. For the first set, differentiate the outcomes by adding content; for the second, differentiate the outcomes by engagement. Which is better? Which is easier? Which would be more appropriate for a future lesson? How do you know?

Like every element of your lesson planning process, learning outcomes will need to be brought to life through your teaching. So, part of the lesson planning process will require you to think about how they become meaningful to every student in your class. Whilst it would be clearly impractical to have detailed learning outcomes written by you for each specific student in each class that you teach, there are important pedagogical strategies such as differentiation and personalisation that you can adopt to meaningfully translate your learning outcomes for the benefit of each student. In Chapter 6 we are going to examine both of these important strategies in more detail.

However, at this point it is important to raise a key point that, perhaps, is one of the most significant in terms of the difference between your early experiences of teaching as part of an initial teacher education course and your work as a full-time member of staff within a school. In the former, you are parachuted into a school for a period of time and expected to take over a selection of classes for a short period. However you are introduced, the students know that you are there training to be a teacher. As a full-time member of staff, you are there for the long term, students respond to you differently and your own sense of identity within the school is considerably stronger. You will be teaching your classes for longer periods of time, perhaps several years, and you will get to know the students within those classes really well. This has a major impact on your ability to plan appropriate learning objectives and outcomes for those classes, perhaps even with specific students in your mind as you do so.

Summary

In this chapter we have introduced the first two key building blocks of a lesson plan: the learning objectives and the learning outcomes. However, we did not start with these. We began by considering three key contexts within which these important elements are situated: your own views about the purposes of education, the broad curricula frameworks that influence your work, and the subject cultures that underpin it. Through this discussion I emphasised how important it was to remain critical and alert to the influences of these formative contexts on your work. They can have a positive and negative impact.

In the second half of the chapter we explored how learning objectives need to focus on the key learning contained within the lesson. They are not a description of activity. They are also deliberately selective and need not cover every aspect of learning that an individual lesson might contain. Learning outcomes need to be written to give an insight into the types of behaviour, skills, attitudes or understanding that might emerge from the teaching activities within a lesson. Written well, they will demonstrate your ability to predict the kinds of learning behaviours that a student who has engaged with the learning objectives that you have set will produce. Written clearly, they provide a handle from which it is possible to assess students' learning effectively.

In the following chapter, we are going to turn our attention to the teaching activities that you might want to include within your lesson. The effective construction of these will be the main way in which your students will be given the opportunity to learn the important lessons that you want to teach.

Further reading

Eisner, E. (2005) 'Expressive learning objectives'. In *Reimagining Schools: The Selected Works of Elliot W. Eisner*. London: Routledge.

In this brilliant chapter, Elliot Eisner contrasts instructional objectives for learning (of the type used routinely in our schools) with expressive learning objectives which can be used to describe an educational encounter. Through their use, Eisner argues, students can be offered an invitation to explore, defer, or focus on issues that are of peculiar interest or import. Expressive learning objectives are evocative rather than prescriptive.

References

Cooper, B. (1983) 'On explaining change in school subjects'. *British Journal of Sociology of Education*, 4:3, 207–222.

DCSF (2008) *The National Curriculum for England*. London: DCSF.

DfE (2013) National curriculum in England: Framework for key stages 1 to 4. www.gov.uk/government/publications/national-curriculum-in-england-framework-for-key-stages-1-to-4/the-national-curriculum-in-england-framework-for-key-stages-1-to-4 (accessed 1 December 2013).

Goodson, I. F. (1991) 'History, context and qualitative methods'. In Goodson, I. F. and Walker, R. (eds) *Biography, Identity and Sociology*. Basingstoke: Falmer Press.

Goodson, I. F. and Mangen, J. M. (1998) 'Subject cultures and the introduction of classroom computers'. In Goodson, I. F. (ed.) *Subject Knowledge: Readings for the Study of School Subjects*. London: Falmer Press.

Jephcote, M. and Davies, B. (2007) 'School subjects, subject communities and curriculum change: The social construction of economics in the school curriculum'. *Cambridge Journal of Education*, 37:2, 207–227.

Sandbach School (2012) http://sandbachschool.org/about-us/mission_values/ (accessed 2 December 2013).

Spear, M., Gould, K. and Lee, B. (2000) *Who Would be a Teacher? A Review of Factors Motivating and Demotivating Prospective and Practising Teachers*. Slough: NFER.

3 The building blocks of a lesson

Introduction

Following the formation of appropriate learning objectives and outcomes (my first two lesson planning stages), the next stage of the lesson planning process is to design engaging teaching activities. These activities will be drawn from a range of sources. However, it is your responsibility to structure them in an appropriate way for the lesson you will be teaching. The key point is to focus the teaching activities in such a way as to engage students and facilitate the key learning outcomes that you have identified.

This chapter will start by examining the main stages within a typical lesson before moving on to consider a range of common types of activities, drawn from numerous subject areas and phases of education. It will also show how key elements such as student curiosity and motivation can be fostered through the design of these teaching activities. Finally, the chapter will examine how teaching activities can be structured within the lesson. Common frameworks will be introduced alongside less common structural devices to help the reader think through the consequences of the structural design of their lesson plan.

Lesson planning stage three: the three-part lesson

Most lessons, regardless of whether they take place in a primary or secondary school, and regardless of what subject content they contain, are built around a few, simple building blocks. At the opening of this chapter, we will consider some of these most common blocks before thinking about how they might be used to 'house' the teaching activities that you are wanting to include within your lesson. As you read through the educational literature, you will find references to a whole range of words that describe these blocks, such as 'starter', 'plenary', the 'three-part' lesson, teaching 'episodes' and other similar terminology.

As you will find out, throughout this book I will be using a number of metaphors to help us unpack the processes involved in effective lesson planning. Perhaps the simplest of these is the obvious metaphorical application of the lesson being like a story. Like all good stories, a good lesson plan needs a beginning, a middle and an end. This simple notion has underpinned a structural framework that has become common in the work of many teachers: the three-part lesson.

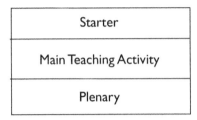

As the name implies, the three-part lesson contains three main stages: starter, main teaching activity and plenary. We will examine each, briefly, in turn. But, first of all, I wish to make it very clear that the three-part lesson is only one potential approach to the design of a lesson. As we will see, there are many others that could be adopted for specific purposes or reasons. However, in my experience as an initial teacher educator, I have found that beginning with the three-part lesson is a very useful and productive starting point for young teachers. Therefore, we will begin with it here.

The starter

The opening of the lesson, the starter, is probably the most important and crucial part of the lesson to get right. Whether students are arriving at your class for their lesson, as in a typical secondary school environment, or you are beginning a new lesson with your class in a primary school context, the opening activities in a new lesson must capture and engage your students' interests immediately. At this point in the lesson, students will be at their most receptive and, if you have done your job properly in creating the appropriate conditions for the beginning of the lesson in terms of your classroom and behaviour management, you will want to capture the energy and expectation of the lesson opening to your advantage.

An effective starter has three main characteristics:

1 Engage all students.

2 Establish the pace of the lesson.

3 Provide challenge.

In one lesson I observed recently, the trainee music teacher had thought hard about an appropriate starter activity. As students entered the room, she had prepared a collection of pictures of musical instruments and other symbols that related to specific elements of music theory that she was teaching the students about. A short extract of music was playing in the background. Displayed on the whiteboard was a simple instruction: choose the pictures of the instruments that you can hear playing and put them together into a timeline that represents the music you can hear. Add musical symbols to illustrate the dynamic contrasts that you can hear.

This starter activity focused around a listening activity. It meant that all students could begin their work immediately on entry to the classroom. There was no waiting around for the lesson to start, no opportunity to get distracted, no opportunity to misbehave. The starter activity contributed to the success of the lesson and key learning objectives within it were picked up later in other activities by the teacher.

In terms of engagement, the example described above shows how vital it is to use the starter to get all students on task quickly. So, this is not the time for lengthy explanations, detailed feedback on a recently completed (or not) homework task, or anything else that will clutter up the opening minutes of the lesson and distract you and them from the key goal of engaging them in a new sequence of learning. You need to make your starter engaging by:

▦ Focusing it explicitly on your learning objective(s).

▦ Ensuring that the task involved in the starter is immediately accessible to all or most students. It needs to be something that the majority of the students in your class do quickly and feel a sense of achievement by completing effectively.

▦ Capturing your students' interests, perhaps through an element of novelty, curiosity or mystery. Your starter activity needs a 'hook' of some sort that has the dual function of engaging your students now, as well as giving you a platform from which to launch the next stage of your lesson.

▦ Making your expectations of what students are to do within the starter explicitly clear and time-bound. This is not the time for an open-ended task that might take a while, with numerous potential outcomes! At this early stage of the lesson, things need to be tight.

▦ Building on what students already know or understand within your subject area. This is a good moment for them to reinforce existing skills but in a new context or to practise or apply subject or generic skills in a new way.

▦ Intervening, when necessary, to help sustain student engagement and ensure that the starter itself does not outlast the concentration span of the students.

As well as being engaging, the starters that you include in your lessons must also be delivered at a good pace. Pace is one of those subjective things that teachers talk about. As a musician and music educator, pace, for me, relates to tempo. Tempo is the flow that underpins a piece of music. It is not so much about the musical details – the melodies, chords, instruments, dynamics – but relates to the underlying movement of the music itself. Within any musical style, whether early Baroque instrumental music or the latest contemporary dance track, this can change in subtle or more obvious ways for expressive effect. As an instrumentalist, listener or dancer, our sense of musical tempo underpins how we respond to a piece of music in a very acute way.

When considering the pace of your lesson, the same elements are true. Pace is not so much about the surface details of the lesson – the words you use, the activities you have chosen, the resources you are using – but rather it is about the underlying feel for the teaching and learning process that you need to be in touch with, and sustain effectively, throughout the lesson. If you are a beginning teacher, you will need to learn to feel how the pace of your lesson is generated and sustained. You will need to watch out for the pace of the lesson slowing too much; this can lead to students disengaging and, in some instances, with consequent problems with student behaviour. As the teacher, you are responsible for ensuring that lessons are delivered at an appropriate pace and, of course, the pace might vary throughout the course of any one individual lesson. Similarly, as with a piece of music, the ways in which your students respond to the lesson pace will vary from individual to individual. There is a lot to watch out for!

So, when I assert that the starter activity of your lesson needs to be delivered at a good pace, what I mean is that the starter itself needs to be delivered purposefully, at a quick pace and with minimal time for students to disengage from the flow of the lesson in those crucial opening minutes. The most common failure that I have seen over the years in the student teachers that I have worked with is that starters can last for too long, sometimes taking over half the lesson! This is wrong but easily correctable. Make sure your starters are just that, starters. They are not the main course. I would suggest that a starter activity should last for around 10% of the allocated lesson time. Within a secondary school context, for example, in a 60-minute lesson I would recommend that the starter activity lasts for somewhere between five and seven minutes only.

But it is important to remember in this discussion about the pace of the starter activity that ensuring your starter has a good pace is not the same as rushing through it. It does mean you move through the starter purposefully, ensuring that distractions are kept to a minimum and that students can be well focused throughout. So, with your starters make sure that:

- ▪ The task is not overly complicated and does not require masses of resources to set up. If possible, make sure all the resources for the starter are in place before your lesson commences. Organisation is key here. As we will see in Chapter 4, preparation is vital and the lesson plan must help you organise your resources in advance of the lesson beginning.

▪ You communicate the key learning objective relating to the starter quickly and simply either before the starter begins or, if you would rather, once the students have engaged with the task by way of summing up and moving on to the main teaching activity.

▪ They are suitably challenging. As with all the building blocks of a lesson, there is a fine line here. The relationship between challenge and engagement needs to be monitored and, as we have seen in our discussion about the pace of the starter, this is particularly important at the beginning of a lesson. If a starter activity is too easy, then students will disengage and get bored; if it is too difficult, frustration will impact on their motivation and could lead to disengagement too. So, simple starters may require students to engage in a particular process, explore a new idea or revise something learnt in a previous lesson; more challenging starters may require them to apply knowledge in a new way, analyse, synthesise or evaluate information or ideas. As the teacher responsible for planning the lesson, it will be vital that you pitch the starter at the right level for your students in that particular lesson. As we have discussed already, lessons do not take place in a vacuum. The broader contextual factors of when the lesson takes place (i.e. the time of day), where it takes place (i.e. the physical space of your classroom) and other factors will all come into play here.

Finally for our discussion on starters, I would like to emphasise that starters need very careful planning. They are a key part of your lesson and vitally important for setting the right tone and expectation for everything that follows after it. Over the last 13 or so years I have watched hundreds of lessons delivered by young teachers. The most successful of these lessons have always included an effective starter activity that has established the tone and direction of the lesson from the start. The lessons that have not gone so well have generally had ineffective starters.

Although it is possible to turn a lesson around after a bad opening, even for experienced teachers this can be a very difficult task. As a beginning teacher, you really need to invest a lot of time in your planning to ensure that lessons start off in the right way. So, for these reasons, make sure that you do the following:

a. Give your starter a clear purpose and relate this to your chosen learning objective.

b. Make the content of the starter engaging and challenging for your students.

c. Deliver your starter at an appropriately brisk pace.

d. Connect the starter to prior or future learning, either by building on what has been learnt in previous lessons or by using it to establish a new idea or topic.

PRACTICAL TASK

Think about a lesson that you are going to teach in the near future. Plan a starter activity in line with the advice given above. Make a written note in your lesson plan to ensure that when you teach the starter, it is done at a brisk pace and does not take more than 10% of the total lesson time available. As the lesson continues, ensure that you refer back to the learning contained within the starter in your comments to the class.

Before we move on to consider the next building block of the three-part lesson, I would like to pick up on the first of these bullet points in a little more detail: the relationship between the opening of the lesson and the presentation of the learning objectives to your students.

In the previous chapter we considered the importance of learning objectives and learning outcomes in planning effectively. One of the key points of that chapter was to stress the centrality of clear learning objectives within the various activities of the lesson. From that approach, and delivery through a skilful pedagogy, students will demonstrate the learning outcomes that you anticipate.

However, in recent years there has been a movement in teaching towards using learning objectives as a structural device within the lesson itself. In my terminology in this chapter, learning objectives have, perhaps, become a building block in their own right. This manifests itself in a number of ways. Learning objectives may be displayed at the commencement of the lesson; students may be asked to write down the learning objectives for the lesson in their planners; teachers may be required to produce 'student friendly' versions of learning objectives as part of their planning; senior managers may insist on learning objectives being verbally communicated to students as part of the opening sequence of a lesson.

When asked, advocates for this approach towards the use of learning objectives state a number of benefits. These include:

a. Students are clear in their minds about what they are being taught.

b. Students are confident that the purpose of the lesson is relevant and timely.

c. Students can measure their own progress towards their achievement of a particular objective.

d. Student behaviour and motivation is better when they have a clear idea of what they are being taught and why.

At a basic level, it is hard to argue with some of these pragmatic and practical benefits. Many of them are self-evident and it would be silly to argue against them. However, there is an alternative view that you need to be aware of.

How do you define teaching? Is it a science, an art, or a craft? Is it a mixture of all three? At various points in the history of education in the United Kingdom, the prevailing view of teaching in educational policy and public life generally has moved between these various perspectives. At the time of writing, there seems to be a view amongst policy makers that teaching is, perhaps, more a craft than an art.

But artistry is central to teaching. As we will see in Chapter 8, the metaphor of the teacher as artist is a powerful one that can help inform and shape our pedagogy. For now, a key part of artistry is the idea of a creative process within which there are elements of surprise. Learning is a creative process. It is hard to predict, in advance, how any one individual student will learn. Whilst broad brushes of learning can be anticipated, the finer details of learning are personal and often hidden from both the student and the teacher. Learning is not limited by time or classroom space; it is a complex network of cognitive, physical, psychological and physiological processes that any one set of learning objectives will almost inevitably fail to capture.

Given this complexity, is the right response to throw up our hands and say that it is impossible to plan for effective learning? No. Effective teaching is about compromises. It is about facilitating the process of learning in a way that leaves the creative learning process open enough for individuals to work within it, facilitating their personal cognitive development and harnessing their intrinsic motivation in meaningful ways. Learning objectives, in this context, need to open up possibilities for learning rather than stifle and close down the sense of the learning journey.

Learning objectives that are used in a dogmatic way to close down the potential avenues of learning should be avoided. Whilst it may be possible to highlight learning objectives in a more positive way, the imposition of learning objectives on students at the beginning of a lesson has a number of negative consequences, including:

- Prioritising what the teacher thinks is important to learn rather than what the students may want to learn.

- Imposing a set of values on different aspects of knowledge that students may, or may not, find difficult to appreciate.

- Removing a sense of surprise or discovery from the lesson that will have a detrimental effect on your students' own intrinsic motivation for learning.

For all these reasons, learning objectives need to be handled very carefully at the beginning of your lesson. Some practical questions need to be asked:

1. Should students be told, in advance, what they are going to learn in a specific lesson?

2. What are the positive and negative consequences of directing students' learning in such an explicit way?

3. What happens if students learn something else instead?

Done uncritically, the inappropriate use of learning objectives can destroy any sense of students being able to undertake a journey within a lesson and discovering new things for themselves. This chapter will challenge your thinking about the pedagogy behind the activities that you build into your lesson plan. Do students need all the information up front, before the starter or main teaching activity begins? Can you drip feed information, knowledge or skills into a learning episode at different points during the lesson?

In Lewis Carroll's *Alice in Wonderland*, Alice and the Cat have a conversation that is often summarised in the following phrase: 'If you don't know where you are going, any road will get you there.' In relation to our discussion here, clearly it is not appropriate within the context of formal schooling for us to have no idea where our students are heading! For all kinds of reasons, not least the fact that experience teaches us the familiarity of particular roads, it is possible to predict in a general sense a direction of travel for our students' experience of learning. However, it is important not to dismiss the potential of alternative directions of travel. Your pedagogical approach to the use of learning objectives as a structural device, or building block, with your lessons needs to be considered very carefully.

REFLECTIVE TASK

Think back on some of the lessons you have observed recently. How were learning objectives handled in those lessons? At what point in the lesson did the teacher communicate these to the students? How was this done? What are the consequences of making learning objectives explicit to students in advance of the lesson being started? If your school has a stated policy in this area, how can you work within this to ensure that the creativity and excitement of discovering new learning is not diminished for your students?

The main teaching activity

Following the starter, the next building block of the three-part lesson is the main teaching activity. Given that your starter will be a short and focused activity and, as we shall see, the plenary should follow the same pattern, this building block will be the longest section of time in your lesson plan. It will also be where the majority of your teaching, and the students' learning, will take place.

Due to the length of this building block, my advice here is to break down this portion of time into specific episodes. As we will see, each episode will probably have its own set of characteristics, function and purpose. But when considered together, all the episodes in this building block will have a sense of coherence and an obvious narrative that will assist your students in achieving the learning outcomes for the lesson that you have planned.

If you are beginning your teaching career, you will soon discover that there is not one single recipe for being a successful teacher. The construction of your main teaching activity, and the various episodes within it, is a highly personal matter. However, there are some key principles that you should abide by.

First, remind yourself about the various contextual factors that are going to influence the lesson itself. These will include the pupils themselves, whether they are taught in a mixed-ability group or have been set (if so how?); whether the class are mixed or single sex; the physical environment of the classroom and the facilities contained therein; the time of the lesson and its placement in the day or week. Second, as you begin to consider your choice of episodes for this building block, commit yourself to a variety of activities. Do not fall into the trap of mono-dimensional teaching (e.g. always telling students things). Rather, make a conscious decision to always include a range of different activities within specific episodes. Your students will enjoy this much more. Finally, every episode should be carefully considered in light of the learning that it will help promote. To this end, ensure that all your episodes, whatever they might entail you and your students doing, can be related closely to the learning objectives that you have established for the lesson (whether or not you have told the students what they might be at this point!).

In Table 3.1, I have drawn together a list of potential episode activities. Against each, I have outlined a basic example drawn from recent lessons I have observed. I hope this will be a useful way to illustrate the rich range of activities that could be adopted within this main teaching activity building block of your three-part lesson.

Table 3.1 Episode activity and examples

Episode activity	Example
Problem-solving	In a design and technology lesson, students were given the raw components for an electrical circuit, including wires, battery, lightbulb and switch. They were asked to assemble the electrical circuit in two contrasting ways for two alternative effects (one obvious and one more obtuse). This required them to think laterally about their components and how they related to each other.
Discussing	In a drama lesson, students were asked to discuss how the characters in a scene that they had previously acted out (which focused on Rosa Parks boarding a bus in Montgomery, Alabama) might have felt. They were asked to empathise with the characters and discuss how their feelings might have been conditioned by the racial segregation laws and broader cultural issues in America at the time.

Table 3.1 Continued

Episode activity	Example
Thinking	In one music lesson students were asked to internalise a number of sounds and imagine them in a number of different permutations. They were asked to compare their abstract thinking in the episode with an alternative approach adopted earlier in the lesson.
Practising	Students were asked to practise their skills of finding the area and perimeter of a rectangle through a sequence of mathematical exercises that made different assumptions and drew on different problem-solving techniques.
Rehearsing	Presenting information concisely and clearly featured in one history lesson, where students had to rehearse a short talk about an interesting historical site that they had recently visited on a field trip.
Performing	The importance of gesture and facial expression was explored in one drama class. Students were asked to perform a short sequence from a play they were studying. During the first run, they used the words of the play; in the second run, they acted it without the words and relied solely on gesture and facial expression to convey meaning to the audience. Students were asked to reflect on their experiences of acting with and without words.
Skill acquisition	During an introduction to long jumping, students were introduced to, and practised, the key skill of positioning the launching foot in the right place on the board. These skills included measuring the run up accurately, which involved making allowance for different stride patterns at speed.
Skill development	In one art lesson students had been considering the skills of shading and texture using pastels. In this class, students developed these skills further through their use of a range of alternative media following an exemplification of these skills by the teacher through his own work.
Divergent thinking	Students seemed to be in a rush to complete a musical composition. The teacher slowed the compositional process down by using a thinking strategy that encouraged the students to find (and dwell on) alternative solutions and approaches for the end of their compositions. Thinking differently (divergently) helped encourage students to find a more convincing end to their own pieces.
Making	Within a food technology class, students were making scones. They were given a number of choices within the task in terms of

Table 3.1 Continued

Episode activity	Example
	ingredients, design and texture. Having made choices, they made the scones and evaluated the results.
Creative work	Students were encouraged to work within a specific creative process to help construct a piece of poetry. This process, although different from the way in which these students normally worked, helped them consider the content of their poems in a new way, challenging their thinking about the purpose and performance of poetry. It led to a fascinating performance piece at the end of the lesson.
Team work	With a rugby lesson, students were encouraged to work together as a group of forwards, supporting and being more receptive to each other's roles within the ruck and maul. In this context, team work included being observant of, and receptive to, the work of others and channelling your own efforts accordingly within the rules of the game.
Drawing	The process of drawing the parameters of a mathematical problem helped the students visualise the mathematical problem set before them in a new way. It externalised some of their internalised thinking and helped the teacher develop a new way of thinking that moved their learning forwards in a helpful direction.
Experimenting	In an English lesson, students were asked to use the outline functions of a word processor to structure their text in four different ways. Experimenting with the flow of the text, via the sequencing of paragraphs, helped them consider the impact of the writing on the specific audience they were writing for.
Writing	Writing and cognitive development are closely linked. In a psychology lesson students were asked to consider how writing with non-digital tools (a pencil or pen) compared to writing with digital tools (a word processor, texting or other mobile technologies).
Reading	In an advanced thinking skills class, students were asked to consider how they read, and how they could develop the skills of speed reading. Different patterns of reading online were explored, including the 'F' or 'T' shaped reading patterns that have been identified by psychologists, before students were given a challenge to test their speed reading and recall abilities.

Table 3.1 Continued

Episode activity	Example
Listening	In a geography lesson, a student was really struggling to grasp the concept of tidal erosion and the movement of physical materials up and down a local coastline. In a one-to-one learning episode, the teacher utilised a new approach to listening and repeating back key information that really seemed to help this student gain an understanding within this topic.
Reflecting	In one music lesson, students were asked to adopt the de Bono 'thinking hats' metaphor to help give a range of feedback to their peers' musical performances.
Speaking	One English teacher was helping her students find their 'voice' in a writing exercise. To assist with this, she asked a number of students to read excerpts from their work to the class. Once verbalised and projected in the classroom space, many of the weaknesses in the narrative became obvious to the students involved.
Communicating	The benefits and pitfalls of alternative communication methods were explored by one ICT teacher. He broadcast a range of instructions to his students in three different ways (through vocal commands, by email and via a website) at the beginning of the lesson. After a (deliberately) slightly chaotic lesson, the teacher revealed the key learning objective of the lesson to the students – every medium of communication has its own strengths and weaknesses.
Valuing	One music teacher found that students did not really value the musical style he was trying to introduce them to. Over a number of learning episodes, week by week, he began to draw more explicit links between the new musical style and those more familiar to the students. By doing so, he was able to shift students' perception of the new musical style by incremental steps.
Forming opinions	How does political rhetoric form opinion? This topic was explored in a lesson on politics. Examples were given from famous political speeches and common devices were unveiled by the teacher, before being utilised by students in a practical exercise.
Analysing	The periodic table classifies the elements in various ways, including according to physical type. Students were asked to analyse a number of unknown chemicals using various methods and identify their constituent elements.

PRACTICAL TASK

Table 3.1 is not exhaustive. There are bound to be many other types of episodes that you could include in your lessons. However, this list does present a number of options that you could begin to use in your own planning. But, as you observe other teachers working, be on the look out for more.

As we have noted in the above examples, some episodes may be more suitable for particular areas of the curriculum than others. However, at this early stage, do not be too worried about this. In fact, it would facilitate your own creative thinking about planning a lesson to work with concepts that are perhaps outside the most obvious episodes that are related to a specific curriculum area or age group.

Within the main teaching activity building block, it is likely that you will want to include several learning episodes. The sequence of these episodes will need to be thought through. Sousa makes an important point about how our memories for particular sequences of learning can be influenced by their position within a particular learning episode:

> During a learning episode, we remember best that which comes first, second best that which comes last, and least that which comes just past the middle . . . The first items of new information are within the working memory's functional capacity so they command our attention, and are likely to be retained in semantic memory. The later information, however, exceeds the capacity and is lost. As the learning episode concludes, items in working memory are sorted or chunked to allow for additional processing of the arriving final items, which are likely held in immediate memory unless further rehearsed. (Sousa 2001, p. 88)

Whilst this is true for the learning contained within a specific episode, it is also true for the learning that is mapped across the sequence of episodes that the main teaching activity contains. So, think carefully about how this important part of the lesson is constructed. Although the sequencing of episodes logically is generally a good strategy, surprising students midway through an episode can be very productive too. Make sure that each learning episode is carefully correlated against the learning objectives you have established for the lesson.

Furthermore, it is important to realise at this stage that the sequence of episodes that you choose may not reflect the sequence of learning that they contain! To illustrate this, consider a simple example like learning to play a scale on the piano. There are certain things that need to be learnt first (e.g. start on this note, then move to this note) and then other ideas can be brought alongside (e.g. use this finger to play this note, this finger to play that note) to aid the fluency of the pianist in playing that particular scale. When students need to learn x before y before z, then the sequence of the episodes and the activities contained therein are relatively easy to establish.

However, if this piano teacher is attempting to teach the young pianist how to use a particular scale within an improvisation on a jazz standard, then things are much more complicated. To begin with, the precise skills to do this activity may not be easily identifiable, and certainly their sequencing will be contested in different approaches towards the teaching of jazz. The context itself, jazz improvisation, brings with it a set of values or attributes that might mitigate against a too rigorous or limited approach. To do so would result in un-musical outcomes that would frustrate the teacher and student alike. Where x is not followed by y, the planning that the teacher needs to do becomes much more sophisticated and should allow for learning to take place in multiple directions.

In either scenario though, a good question to ask yourself as a teacher is this: what is the minimum amount of information or instruction that a student needs before they can have a go at something themselves? Young teachers often fall into the trap of talking too much, or of thinking that they need to cover all the information, up front, in a particular main teaching activity. This is not necessary. By conceptualising the main teaching activity as a series of episodes, you can begin to break down the sequence of learning in to manageable chunks. Make it your aim to talk less and get your students to do more!

The episodes that you put together within your main teaching activity should be full of activities for the students to engage in. Regardless of the age of the students, the subject, the curriculum focus or theme, these teaching and learning activities should be:

- *Purposeful*: you should always know what the main learning objective behind the activity is and this should be communicated to students at some point during the episode (not always at the beginning!).

- *Dynamic*: all activities should involve the students in doing something active (either physically or cognitively) and should involve a range of episode activity as discussed above.

- *Differentiated*: it should give all students a chance to be challenged and, hopefully, successful at a level appropriate to their abilities. We will consider this aspect further in Chapter 6.

- *Time limited* and *sequenced*: each activity should have a clear time limit and the links between episodes that contain the activities should be carefully planned to ensure progression from one episode to the next.

That said, episodes and their activities should also be varied in different ways. This is important. You do not want to become a 'one trick' teacher and surprising your students is a good way of challenging their thinking and motivating their learning.

So, when designing episodes for your main teaching activity, you will need to think about many different things.

First, consider the location of the main teaching activity. Are you always restricted to the immediate classroom environment? On the majority of occasions you probably will be, but there will be times when it could be delivered in a different space that might facilitate a different form of interaction between you and your students. If you cannot move the class easily to an alternative space, what would happen if you rearrange the space in the classroom itself? How would this change the ways in which students interact between themselves within the episode?

Second, think about the group structure for the episode. Are students going to be working individually, in pairs or small groups within the episode? What difference would it make if you adopted an alternative grouping? Whilst some activities might be suited to individual approaches, you can challenge students' ways of thinking by situating the activity in a different grouping. As we will see in the Mosston and Ashworth (2002) taxonomy below, there are numerous different approaches in teaching style that could have beneficial consequences. The construction of groups is also worth considering. There are many alternatives here, including grouping students by ability, gender, friendship or age. You can also scaffold the group work for a specific activity in different ways – for example, by providing roles for particular students to play, or designating different ways of viewing the activity. As we discussed above in our list of teaching episodes, de Bono's thinking hats is one example of this kind of approach (see www.debonothinkingsystems.com/tools/6hats.htm for further details on this).

Third, always consider the flow and pace of the lesson and the role that carefully chosen episodes can play in maintaining this. New episodes can be introduced that interrupt and re-point a main teaching activity in a different direction, perhaps by introducing a new challenge for a group, or reassigning the roles of the group in order to challenge students' thinking at key moments. All of this, and more, can help make the main teaching activity within your lesson varied and exciting for your students.

Next, the resources that students need to complete an activity within an episode need careful thought. As we will see in the next chapter, at a cognitive and psychological level, the tools that we provide for a particular activity will fundamentally alter the types of thinking and learning that our students are able to engage in. For example, working through long division in mathematics with a calculator facilitates a different type of mathematical thinking from working with a pencil and paper (see Wertsch 1998, especially chapter 2, for a fantastic exploration of these ideas).

Furthermore, the time allocated for the activity needs careful consideration. Recently, I have noticed that there seems to be a move towards including shorter, more targeted, teaching activities within lesson plans. This is fine as far as it goes. But you should not forget that some things take time and are worthy of contemplation (by students and teachers). Long activities are still worthwhile and can help teach students the skills of independent learning when scaffolded appropriately. However, you will need to ensure that sustaining student motivation is at the forefront of your mind if you are going to include longer episodes in your lesson plan.

On this point, it is interesting to read the reflections of key educational thinkers on their own teachers. One such example is Professor Robin Alexander's recollections of Douglas Brown, a teacher of English at the Perse School in Cambridge during the 1950s and 1960s (Alexander 2008, pp. 154–72). Alexander writes:

> His manner of engaging with language and literature, and his close attention to words written and spoken, are with me to this day. His intellect, insight, skill and independence make today's ministerial accolades for politically compliant 'best practice' look utterly tawdry. His moral but never moralistic engagement with literature, music and life render irresponsible as well as contemptible the UK government's injunction to sue the dismal pragmatism of 'what works' as the sole touchstone for defining good teaching. (Ibid., p. 171)

Teaching has changed dramatically in recent years. However, not all of this change has been for the better. It is important to remember that great teaching in our past looked very different from what teaching is like today. Alexander continues:

> His high educational ambitions for his pupils were quite unlike today's teaching 'targets' because we made them our own, gladly, willingly and without the crude panoply of pressures, threats and sanctions upon which the post-1997 target-setting apparatus has depended. In any case, targets may be intended to raise horizons but actually they impose limits and Douglas's aspirations certainly did not. Indeed, they probably far exceeded any targets or attainment levels that might have been thought appropriate to students of the ages he taught – not that we achieved them; aiming high was what mattered. (Ibid.)

Alexander's recollections of Douglas Brown are many and varied. Not least amongst them are the skills of oratory, of using language – both written and spoken – to engage with young people and draw them into new worlds of literacy, the arts and music. There are important lessons here for teachers of all ages and expertise. Jumping on a political bandwagon of 'what works' should always be avoided, whatever the cost. Teachers can talk at length in lessons, but make sure that you talk well.

This leads us on to another important consideration. What is your practical role in all of this? What will you be doing if you are not talking all the time? Before we consider the third stage of our three-part lesson, let us take a short diversion into the areas of 'teaching style' and 'teaching role' and see how they relate to your planning for these episodes.

Different writers and thinkers on teaching have spent many pages writing about teaching style and role. We will consider two main sets of ideas here. First, Mosston and Ashworth (2002) produced a taxonomy of teaching styles (Table 3.2). Many of these will be fairly familiar to anyone who has spent more than a few hours watching teaching within a school.

Table 3.2 Teaching styles

Teaching style	Meaning
Command	Teacher-centred exposition, 'chalk and talk', the type of which we have all experienced but needs to be done in small doses.
Practice	The teacher sets tasks for students to practise throughout the episode.
Reciprocal	Students work in pairs, with one student giving feedback to the other. This can be applied to group work too.
Self-check	The teacher establishes success criteria and the students work at their own level against these.
Inclusion	The teacher sets a range of tasks and students choose which they want to work on. (Please note that their use of this term is slightly different from current usage.)
Guided discovery	The teacher guides the learner towards a predetermined outcome using questions and tasks within the learning episode.
Convergent discovery	One outcome required, with the teacher guiding, if needed, their students towards this one outcome.
Divergent discovery	There are many outcomes possible, and the teacher supports, if needed, their students towards discovering one outcome (which may be very different from other students in the class).
Learner designed	The teacher decides the topic area; the student chooses their own programme of study within it.
Learner initiated	The student decides what they wish to learn and organises how they will do it with the support of the teacher if needed.
Self-teach	Entirely independent with no teacher participation.

Knowing that your actions as a teacher can vary, episode by episode, can help you consider a range of approaches within the main teaching activity sequence of your lesson. Try to develop a variety of approaches in any one lesson. Importantly, make sure that you have time to step back and observe what is going on at some point. This can be a vital opportunity to help you gather evidence for your assessment of the learning that is taking place (something that we will explore in more detail in Chapter 5).

The second taxonomy we will consider relates to teaching role. Stephen Downes' research has identified multiple roles that a teacher could play out within their classes. These are presented in Table 3.3 together with a brief explanation summarised from his work (Downes 2013).

Table 3.3 Teaching roles

Teacher roles	Explanation
The Learner	'As someone who models the act of learning, the teacher helps students with this most fundamental of skills. This includes getting exited about something new, exploring it, trying it out and experimenting, engaging with it and engaging with others learning about it.'
The Collector	'Teachers have always been collectors, from the days when they would bring stacks of old magazines into class to the modern era as they share links, resources, new faces and new names. They find materials related to their own interests, keep in tune with student interests. They are the maven, the librarian, the journalist or the archivist.'
The Curator	'The curator is one who organises and makes sense of that which has been found. The curator is like a caretaker and a preserver, but also a creator of meaning, guardian of knowledge, or an expert at knowing. A curator is a connoisseur, one who brings quality to the fore, one who sequences and presents.'
The Alchemist	'The alchemist mixes the ordinary and mundane into something new and unexpected. The alchemist practices the "mix" of remix, the "mash" of mash-up, the "collage" of bricolage. The alchemist sees patterns and symmetries in distinct materials and brings them together to bring that out.'
The Programmer	'The programmer builds sequences into machines, manipulates symbols to produce meaning, calculates, orders, assembles, and manages.'
The Salesperson	'The salesperson plays an important role in providing information, supporting belief and motivating action. The salesperson is the champion of a cause or an idea.'
The Convener	'The convenor is the person who brings people together. A convener is a network builder, a community organiser. Conveners are leaders, coaches, and administrators; they are collaboration builders, coalition builders, enablers or sometimes even just pied pipers.'
The Coordinator	'The coordinator organises the people or things that have been brought together for the common good. A coordinator is an eminently practical person, organising schedules, setting expectations, managing logistics, following up and solving problems. A coordinator is a connector and an integrator, but most of all, a systems person.'

Table 3.3 Continued

Teacher roles	Explanation
The Designer	'The purpose of the designer is to create spaces for learning, whether they are in person, on paper or online. They attend to flow, perspectives, light, tone and shading.'
The Coach	'The coach does everything from creating synergy and chemistry in a group to providing the game plan for learning, raising the bar and encouraging players to higher performance. Though the coach is on the side of the learner, in the learner's corner urging them on and giving advice, the coach also serves a larger or higher objective, working to achieve team or organisational goals.'
The Agitator	'The agitator is the person who creates the itch a person's education will eventually scratch. The role of the agitator is to create the seed of doubt, the sense of wonder, the feeling of urgency, the cry of outrage. The agitator is sometimes the devil's advocate, sometimes the revolutionary, sometimes the disruptive agent, and sometimes just somebody who is thinking outside the box.'
The Facilitator	'The facilitator makes the learning space comfortable. Their role is to cover the process or move the conversation forward, but within a broad range of parameters that will stress clarity, order, inclusiveness, and good judgment. The facilitator keeps things on track and within reason, gently nudging things forward, but without typically imposing his or her opinions or agenda onto the outcome.'
The Moderator	'The moderator governs and prunes. The moderator of a forum is concerned about decorum, good behaviour and rules. He or she will tell people to "shush" while the movie is playing, trim the trolls from the discussion thread, and gently suggest that the experienced pro ought to go more easily on the novice.'
The Critic	'The critic is the person who asks for evidence, verifies the facts, assesses the reasoning, and offers opinions. They are an aide to understanding, one who will extract the threads of a tangled presentation and make them clear. As logic texts everywhere proclaim, criticism consists first of exposition and only then of examination.'
The Lecturer	'The lecturer has the responsibility for organising larger bodies of work or thought into a comprehensible whole, employing the skills of rhetoric and exposition to make the complex clear for the listener or reader.'

Table 3.3 Continued

Teacher roles	Explanation
The Demonstrator	'Demonstration has always been a part of education, whether a carpenter demonstrating proper mitering to an apprentice or a chemist demonstrating proper lab technique to a class. Traditionally, demonstration has been done in person, but today people who demonstrate can use actual equipment, simulations, or video to tell their stories.'
The Mentor	'The role of mentor is itself multi-faceted, ranging from sharp critic to enthusiastic coach, but outweighing these is the personal dimension, the presence of the entire personality rather than some domain or discipline. Not everyone can be a mentor, not every mentor can take on too many prodigies, and of all the roles described here, that of the mentor is most likely to be honorary or voluntary.'
The Connector	'The connector draws associations and makes inferences. The connector is the person who links distinct communities with one another, allowing ideas to flow from art to engineering, from database design to flower arranging. The connector sees things in common between disparate entities and draws that line between them, creating links and collaborations between otherwise isolated communities and disciplines. The connector sees emergent phenomena, patterns across different groups or different societies, or conversely, identifies the unusual, unique or unexpected.'
The Theoriser	'The theoriser tries to describe how or why something is the case. The theoriser often works through abstraction and generalisation, which leads to critics saying he or she is not very practical, but without the theoriser we would have no recourse to very useful unseen phenomena such as mass, gravity or information. The theoriser is also the person who leads us to develop world views, finds the underlying cause or meaning of things, or creates order out of what appears to be chaos.'
The Sharer	'The sharer shares material from one person to another on a systematic basis. The sharer might be the person making e-Portfolios available, the person managing the class mailing list, or the person passing along links and reflections from outside. But ultimately, what the sharer offers most are cultures, concepts and ideas.'

Table 3.3 Continued

Teacher roles	Explanation
The Evaluator	'The evaluator is more than a marker of tests and assigner of grades; the evaluator does not merely assess declarative knowledge or compositional ability, but instinct and reactions, sociability, habits and attitudes.'
The Bureaucrat	'The bureaucrat provides the statistics so much needed by the coordinator, manages the finances and resources, tracks the services needed by facilitators, organises accountability procedures and maintains systemic coherence.'

REFLECTIVE TASK

So, what kind of teacher are you? Which of Downes' roles did you think best described your own work? Which one describes the work of other teachers who have taught you, or perhaps you have seen teaching recently? More importantly, how do you think that specific roles that Downes' identifies could help you structure particular teaching episodes and the activities that they contain?

It is probably the case for most of us that we will recognise a number of these roles within our personality and role as a teacher. However, like any taxonomy, it does challenge us to think about our comfort zone and imagine things differently. What would it be like to be the 'teacher as agitator'? How could I develop my teaching so I bring more of the 'teacher as alchemist' to the fore? Questions such as these will help you think differently about your role within the classroom; this will begin to have a bearing on how you start to plan particular teaching episodes and re-imagine your role within them.

Whichever taxonomy you find useful, the teaching styles or the teaching roles, they both present a very helpful array of different approaches to your work within your classroom. As with the episodes and their sequence within the main teaching activity of your three-part lesson, there is no right or wrong answer here. Rather, taxonomies like these equip you with a range of particular options that you can explore within your pedagogy. I would advise you not to become too dependent on any one approach. Adopt a playful approach to your teaching style and role, draw on multiple ideas and approaches within the learning episodes that you construct within your plan. Therein lies one of the keys to a sustained and enjoyable teaching career. We will return to some of these ideas in Chapter 8 when we consider what is meant by the 'performance' of teaching. For now, we are going to turn our attention to the final part of the traditional three-part lesson.

Plenaries

The word 'plenary' comes from the Latin word *plenarius*, meaning 'full' or 'full-ness'. In the traditional three-part lesson, the plenary is the final section of the lesson. It completes the lesson and provides a meaningful sense of closure for the students and teacher alike.

The key function of the plenary is to bring to a close the learning that has taken place in the lesson. In recent years, plenaries have become recognised as an essential strategy by which teachers can develop and value the students' role in assessment. Whilst the summing up of learning objectives, the analysis of learning outcomes, and the signposting of new learning (all of which are important elements of an effective plenary) were undoubtedly appreciated as an effective way of teaching long before the various National Strategies were developed during the 1990s (of which Alexander was so scathing), the adoption of these strategies through the early part of the twenty-first century has consolidated the notion of the plenary as an essential part of a lesson plan within both primary and secondary schooling.

Normally plenaries take place at the end of a lesson. However, as the observant reader will notice, I have not called this section 'The plenary' for a reason. There is good evidence to suggest that the adoption of 'mini-plenaries' throughout a lesson can have a positive impact on students' learning. These can help you draw together all the various strands of a specific learning episode in a helpful way. Here, the plenary is a moment of summary before further action begins.

Plenaries have many characteristics including:

- Drawing together the whole group and providing a helpful sense of community as the lesson closes.

- Helping the group of students summarise and take stock of the learning that has been achieved both individually and corporately.

- Providing opportunities for the extension of learning through homework or other learning opportunities.

- Signposting future learning in the next lesson or teaching episode.

- Highlighting not only what pupils have learnt but also how they have learnt it.

Many plenaries that I observe in lessons include a lot of questions. But teacher-directed plenaries that involve asking a lot of questions are seldom going to be very effective as plenaries. The most effective plenaries that I have observed are when the teacher asks the students to engage in an activity that re-contextualise the key learning objectives of the lesson in a different way through a stimulating activity. In one recent example from an English lesson I observed, the teacher was exploring the various ways in which different characters were portrayed by Shakespeare in his play *Romeo and Juliet*. Key learning objectives relating to two characters had been developed through the lesson. In the plenary, the teacher asked her students to work in pairs and to take these key lessons from their study of Shakespeare's work and to apply them to the development of two characters in a short piece of improvised drama. This simple transposition of the key techniques of characterisation allowed students a significant degree of creative freedom that they really enjoyed and the lesson ended on a very positive note. It also allowed the teacher the opportunity to observe the impact of the learning objectives on students' work in a different domain (physical theatre) rather than solely being reliant on the written word.

The key point that I want to emphasise here is that to run an effective plenary, either at the end of the lesson or at a strategic point within the lesson, you have to place the students' learning experiences at the heart of a dialogue that you need to facilitate. This dialogue might take place between you and the students, or it might take place between the students themselves, or it might take place between an individual student and a reflective mechanism such as a journal.

From my observations of lessons over the years, plenaries become problematic when the teacher remains in control in a dictatorial sense, talks too much, simply sees the plenary as another opportunity to restate the learning objectives that were established earlier in the lesson, or does not communicate the purpose and function of the plenary to the students in a considered way.

Effective plenaries need to place the student at the heart of the assessment process. This is something that we will consider in more detail in Chapter 5. For now, some of the following simple principles will help you construct a meaningful plenary for your lesson plan:

- Give students prior knowledge of the plenary and the types of questions that you are going to be asking them to consider. You can do this at a very early stage of the lesson if your planning process has been rigorous and precise.

- Extend the feedback that students give you by using supplementary or extension questions. Try to avoid low-level reiteration of basic ideas. This is a difficult skill and it may not come easily. So, in advance of the lesson, plan key supplementary questions and write these down in your lesson plan. Refer to this during the plenary, if necessary, to help you move away from the simple repetition of basic content that you are trying to avoid.

- Ensure that the plenary continues to progress the learning rather than merely summarising it. Key signposting of future learning can also be a helpful way to motivate students and maintain their motivation at the end of the lesson.

- Try to vary the routine of your plenaries. They will not always involve questions and answers. Take another look at the episode activities that I outlined earlier in this chapter. Many of these can be used and applied to plenaries in the same way that we considered them as episodes within the main teaching activity. Think about how you can build visual or kinaesthetic activities within the plenary so that it is not solely about a verbal conversation. Try to be imaginative in the plenary's structure and process.

■ Develop a conceptual map of the plenary for your own assessment processes. This will help you immensely as you begin the process of evaluating your lessons (of which much more will be discussed in Chapter 9).

Summary

This chapter has introduced a number of simple ideas related to the building blocks of the three-part lesson. Right at the beginning of the chapter I emphasised that the three-part lesson, of the type described here, is not the only format that a lesson can take. As this book proceeds, you will find references to several other different formats for lessons (particularly when we consider issues related to documentation in Chapter 7).

However, even within this chapter we can see that a simple model for a three-part lesson such as this:

Starter

Main Teaching Activity

Plenary

. . . can turn into something a little more complex, like this:

Starter
Main Teaching Activity
Episode 1
Episode 2
Mini-plenary
Episode 3
Episode 4
Plenary (full)

This simple approach to a three-part lesson gives you plenty of ideas for starting teaching. Throughout the chapter, I have also made some explicit links to different aspects of your pedagogy – your teaching style and your teaching role. These broader aspects of your own teaching are very closely linked to your planning processes. One of the key arguments throughout this book is that planning and pedagogy go hand in hand. It is a theme to which we will return in each of the following chapters.

Further reading

Eisner, E. (2002) *The Arts and the Creation of Mind.* New Haven and London: Yale University Press.

This is the book that I recommend most highly to my students. Although it deals with the arts in education, it is also highly appropriate for all students undertaking initial teacher education programmes (and for established teachers). I recommend it here because within this book Eisner addresses directly many of the issues that I have explored in this chapter in greater detail.

References

Alexander, R. (2008) *Essays on Pedagogy.* London: Routledge.

Downes, S. (2013) The role of the educator. www.huffingtonpost.com/stephen-downes/the-role-of-the-educator_b_790937.html (accessed 2 October 2013).

Mosston, M. and Ashworth, S. (2002) *Teaching Physical Education* (5th edition). San Francisco: B. Cummings.

Sousa, D. A. (2001) *How the Brain Learns: A Classroom Teacher's Guide* (2nd edition). Thousand Oaks, CA: Corwin Press.

Wertsch, J. (1998) *Mind as Action.* Oxford: Oxford University Press.

4 Resourcing the lesson

Introduction

In the previous chapter, we explored some of the common building blocks of a typical lesson structure. Using the three-part lesson as your starting point, you can begin to sequence teaching activities in episodes to help students achieve the learning objectives and learning outcomes that you have set for them. In this chapter, our attention is going to turn to some of the other things that you will need to consider thinking about in relation to your lesson plan. Classroom resources can take many different shapes or forms. They include subject-specific items such as musical instruments or scientific measuring devices, or generic technologies such as the interactive whiteboard or simple colouring pencils. Whatever form they take, it is crucial that you consider carefully both your choice of resources for a lesson and how students will use them to achieve the particular learning objectives and outcomes you have planned.

This chapter will begin with a short discussion about 'mediated action' drawn from the work of James Wertsch (1998). Following on from this, we will explore a number of common, practical examples of classroom resources that you will have to consider in your teaching, whether you are a primary or secondary school teacher. These will include the classroom space itself, the use of classroom displays, digital technologies and opportunities for the constructive use of outside spaces and their resources for learning. The chapter will conclude by looking at how important it is for you to build a resource network of your own to support your teaching.

A framework for mediated action in teaching and learning

What is mediated action?

All teaching involves us doing things. When asked what teachers do, many young children say that they talk a lot! And, of course, the vast majority of teaching does involve language, whether it is spoken or written. But teaching also includes physical actions that take place within specific physical environments (class-rooms) and involve various other physical or virtual objects (the 'resources'). These environments have been formed over many years and often take on a common 'look' that will help us, instinctively, feel at home within them. Of course, human action is a fundamental dimension of every part of our lives and, as such, the actions that we make and the specific contexts within which they occur have been subjected to considerable analysis by sociologists and psychologists. One writer, James Wertsch (1998), has explored the link between actions and their context in a very sophisticated way. He defines the task of this type of analysis as being:

> To explicate the relationship between human action, on the one hand, and the cultural, institutional, and historical contexts in which this action occurs, on the other. (Ibid., p. 24)

Wertsch defines this link between action and context as 'mediated action'. For him, all human action is mediated action. Mediated action takes place in a particular context (or scene), against a particular backdrop, with particular characters involved (who he calls 'agents'), who use particular tools and interact with particu-lar sets of ideas and assumptions. All these features mediate the actions we take, sometimes explicitly and sometimes implicitly, sometimes internally and some-times externally.

Within his book, Wertsch's own exposition of the theme of 'mediated action' draws on many examples, including the QWERTY keyboard and approaches to long division. Another example, perhaps more surprising but no less illuminating, comes from the athletics field.

Pole-vaulting has a long history (Rosenbaum 2009). The first known pole-vault competitions were held during the Irish Tailteann Games, which date back as far as 1829 BC. The sport became an Olympic event in 1896. Central to the sport of pole-vaulting is the pole! Wertsch defines the pole as an example tool, a type of resource. But in the history of pole-vaulting, this tool and the materials from which it has been made have been the source of many problems.

Early poles were made of wood. They were probably just large sticks or tree limbs. In the nineteenth century, competitors developed these primitive objects into wooden poles, but these were replaced by bamboo (lighter and a little bit more flexible) prior to the Second World War. Subsequent developments saw the emergence of metal poles (which were obviously stronger) and then aluminium poles (stronger and lighter). Today, the modern pole-vaulting athlete has the benefit of carbon-fibre and fibreglass composite poles (which are lighter, stronger and more flexible). Despite the changes in the materials used to make the pole, the aim of pole-vaulting has remained the same: to get over the highest possible barrier. In that first 1896 appearance of pole-vaulting in the Olympic Games, William Hoyt won with a leap of 3.30m; the current world record of 6.14m was set by Sergey Bubka in 1994.

Wertsch's more detailed account of these developments (1998, pp. 27–8) charts the various rivalries and factions within the pole-vaulting community that emerged at transition points surrounding the adoption of new poles. At one point these even included the possibility of breakaway groups favouring a particular type of pole, and accusations that users of new types of poles were cheating. The history of pole-vaulting itself distinguishes between the various 'eras' of particular poles (Rosenbaum 2009).

As a tool or resource, the pole is essential to pole-vaulting. It mediates the action between the athlete (the agent) and the goal of hurtling over the barrier at the highest possible height (the context). By using techniques of sociocultural analysis, Wertsch's chapter goes on to explore the relationship between human actions and the cultural, institutional and historical contexts in which this action occurs. In our context, teachers or pupils are the 'agents' (to use Wertsch's terminology), the 'cultural tools' are the resources we are choosing to use within are teaching, and the context would be, at least in a simple application of his work, your classroom or other learning spaces where students can work both formally and informally. Wertsch calls the interplay between agents (you and your students), tools (your classroom resources) and contexts (your teaching) 'mediated action'.

Mediated action and teaching

In the previous section we explored Wertsch's key assertion that all human action is mediated action. Applying this to our discussion, all teaching and learning involves mediated action. Our teaching is mediated by the resources that we choose to use; our students' formal and informal learning is mediated by the resources they choose to use. These resources will take many different forms. They will include the spoken and written language that we use within the classroom, but they will also include elements such as the curriculum framework we are working within, the physical classroom space itself, what is contained within that space, other resources such as books, digital technologies and other objects, the displays and much more besides.

The learning objectives that we set for a particular lesson, and the learning outcomes that are exhibited by our students, can all be viewed within this wider conceptual framework of mediated action. So just as you can jump higher within pole-vaulting with certain types of poles, so you can aim for different learning outcomes through the effective use of different resources. Similarly, it may be possible to aim for more challenging, complex teaching and learning if the resources that you have chosen to use allow your students to take care of basic, lower-level functions or issues and concentrate on other things. The point here is that all these potential resources exist within a wider network of teaching, learning and cognitive processes. Within this network, your key role will be to seek to understand and to exploit the possible educational affordances offered by particular resources. This is what this chapter will try to help you obtain.

PRACTICAL TASK

Make a list of as many resources that you can think of that you use regularly in your teaching. Make sure that you include cognitive as well as physical resources. You will need this list for future tasks in this chapter.

Key principles of mediated action

Wertsch goes on to list the ten key properties of mediated action. These are summarised in Table 4.1, together with some short comments that I hope will help you understand how the specific principle relates to the general theme of this chapter.

Table 4.1 Wertsch's ten principles of mediated action applied to teaching and learning

Wertsch's principle	Exemplification
1 Mediated action is characterised by an irreducible tension between agents and mediational means.	Resources are powerless to do anything in and of themselves. They can have their impact only when you use them in a particular way.
2 Mediational means are material.	The material properties of a resource have important implications for how the teacher or student may use it, and how we (as teachers) seek to understand how our students' understanding is developed by their using that resource.
3 Mediated action typically has multiple simultaneous goals.	Mediated action often includes multiple and conflicting goals. Your, or your students', goals for the use of a particular resource may conflict with other mediational means that the resource itself presents.
4 Mediated action is situated on one or more developmental paths.	You, your students and the resources that you choose to use in your teaching all have a past and are always in the process of undergoing further change. Therein can lie unresolved (but often productive) tensions that can be explored.
5 Mediational means constrain as well as enable action.	Our use of resources can be empowering and enabling. But it can also constrain or limit the forms of action we undertake. You need to be open to both possibilities.

Table 4.1 Continued

Wertsch's principle	Exemplification
6 New mediational means transform mediated action.	The dynamics of change caused by introducing new resources for mediated action are powerful and must be considered carefully.
7 The relationship of agents towards mediational means can be characterised in terms of mastery.	The emphasis needs to be on how you and your students use a particular resource skilfully. Focusing on how a resource facilitates generalised abilities or aptitudes is unlikely to get the best out of your students.
8 The relationship of agents towards mediational means can be characterised in terms of appropriation (i.e. taking something that belongs to others and making it one's own).	Resources are not easily and smoothly 'appropriated' by teachers or students. Some form of resistance or friction is the rule rather than the exception. So how can you seek to build on this and understand the consequences for teaching and learning?
9 Mediational means are often produced for reasons other than to facilitate mediated action.	Most of the resources we employ in our teaching were not designed for that purpose. So what compromises need to be made by us and our students?
10 Mediational means are associated with power and authority.	Where is the power and authority situated in your classroom? A focus on mediated action and the resources employed in your classroom will allow you to explore action, power, and authority in a new and helpful way.

Up to this point, this chapter has explored a theoretical model drawn from social-cultural theory that will help you understand how resources are situated within your classroom. My suggestion here is that the mediated actions that result from your inclusion of specific resources within that classroom space, both by you and by your students, is worthy of study and analysis. It will help you understand more fully how teaching and learning is facilitated; it will also help you plan more effectively for learning. Put simply, choosing your resources, being able to justify their selection, and planning for their use skilfully and carefully for the teaching episodes that you are designing is an essential skill of the effective teacher.

PRACTICAL TASK

Take your list from the previous practical task. For each item on it, can you justify the selection of the individual resource through what it facilitates as a tool in the teaching and learning context? Can you begin to identify some of the limitations of each individual resource as well as the potential benefits?

We will now turn our attention to some practical examples of resources that you will find in your classroom. We will start with the most obvious – the classroom environment itself, before turning our attention to other resources, technologies and people that we often find within it. At the end of the chapter, we will briefly be considering how teaching and learning can be facilitated in other areas outside the traditional classroom before turning our attention back on to you, the teacher, and the resources that you need to sustain and develop your role.

Lesson planning stage four: the classroom environment

The classroom that you teach in is one of the most important resources that you have at your disposal. How it is designed, the position of the furniture, the location of presentational technologies, the wall displays, the way it is lit and so much more will influence the activities that take place within it. For many beginning teachers, you will be teaching in someone else's classroom. You will have little if any say about the design of the room, nor will you be able to change many of its key features such as the position of tables, chairs or the classroom displays. In many schools today, teachers will be regularly working in many different classroom spaces. They may not have their 'own' classroom as such, unlike the teachers of previous generations. But, even so, it is important to think about the classroom space that you are teaching in, whether it is your own classroom or not, and how it will impact on how you plan for the teaching and learning that will occur there.

Many schools have specialist teaching spaces where certain subjects are taught. Science laboratories, art rooms, design workshops and other spaces all have certain features that facilitate particular forms of action in a helpful way. I have heard of certain teachers having to teach their own subject – for example, Music – within a specialist space such as a science laboratory. When careless timetabling of this sort takes place, it challenges the subject teacher (in this case the Music teacher) to re-conceptualise the way in which they might be able to teach their subject. Clearly, in this case, the teacher might have considered having to teach music in a science laboratory unhelpful. But it does prove how important the classroom space is in determining our actions.

Generally, teaching spaces have not changed significantly over the last 100 years. They are still dominated by one type of design which will be very familiar to you. It is:

tutor-focused, one way facing and presentational, with seating arranged in either a U-shape or in straight rows. Technologies have subsequently been added – interactive or conventional whiteboards mounted on the wall behind the main speaker, ceiling-mounted projectors with cabling to a laptop, a wireless network and/or wired computers – but these have rarely altered the dynamics of the design. (JISC 2006, p. 10)

As we have seen already, this traditional design does not lend itself to change very easily. But it is essential that through your lesson planning process you consider the space carefully. The Design Council comment that:

> The environment can only make a difference if it is used by creative teachers with an appropriate curriculum and resources. Yet for many teachers their environment is still a blind spot: unchanging, unchangeable and beyond their control – an obstacle that they must work around, rather than a tool to support and enhance their practice. (Design Council 2005, p. 18)

Do not allow this 'blind spot' to develop. Even if the classroom space is not easily adaptable, the process of thinking through the consequences of the design of the existing space on your work as a teacher will make a significant difference to how you plan your lessons. Work hard at imagining the lesson in that space. Ask yourself basic questions such as:

- Where will I be standing for key points during the lesson? (I would not suggest that you ever teach sitting down.)

- Where will the students be sitting?

- If students need to move, will they be able to do this easily (quickly and safely)?

- Does the location of other key resources (e.g. presentational technologies) facilitate the process of teaching and learning within the space?

- Are other resources easily accessible, by me or by the students, within the design of the classroom space?

At some point, hopefully, you will be in a position to influence the design and organisation of a classroom space for your own teaching. This is a great privilege and will allow you the opportunity to really consider how the classroom in its entirety can help you develop your teaching even further.

So, the organisation of the classroom space is an integral part of your planning and pedagogy. The organisation of the elements within that context will play a part in shaping what occurs. Recent research has considered the design of alternative spaces for teaching and learning in our schools. It has suggested a number of key features that need to be included:

1 Accommodating the formation and function of small learning groups alongside more traditional approaches to pedagogical instruction. When groups work they

need a degree of separation within a space otherwise they will become distracted; therefore . . .

2 Classroom space needs to be flexible to allow for the easy reorganisation of the class into groups; but . . .

3 The space needs to be managed by a single teacher so they need to be positioned appropriately and the space needs to be compact and open. (McGregor 2007, p. 18)

In light of these suggestions, here are some specific questions related to common resources found in a typical classroom. Work through these questions whenever you are faced with working in a new classroom environment. As part of your planning, consider how each of your key building blocks and teaching episodes will be facilitated or limited by the various physical resources of the classroom space itself.

Tables and chairs

- How are these organised in your classroom?

- Are they in rows or lines?

- Are they easily moved?

- What would happen if you got rid of them completely?

- How would that affect the way that you teach?

- Would it matter if your students did not have anything to write on?

- What would they do instead?

Blackboard, whiteboard or interactive whiteboard

- Where are these situated?

- What type of teaching style do these technologies facilitate?

- How do you use them in a typical lesson?

- How do they implicate the way in which your class is organised (i.e. where they sit in order to see the board)?

We will consider the role and function of classroom displays in more detail below.

Finally in this section on the classroom environment, there are two important wider issues associated with the organisation of the classroom space. First, health and safety issues need to be taken into consideration at all times. Whilst the traditional classroom layout could be seen to mitigate these concerns, do not be complacent. If you are considering changes to established layouts of tables and chairs or other resources, do consider the health and safety implications. If, as we will explore below, you are considering bringing new resources into the classroom space, then similarly careful strategies for their use need to be planned.

Second, the management of student behaviour is closely linked to the physical environment. Whilst it is beyond the scope of this book to go into a lot of detail about this, do reflect for a moment on why certain physical classroom environments are designed the way they are. Therein lies a number of clues about the management of student behaviour within those spaces. One classic example concerns the layout of computer suites. In the early days of computer laboratories, the computers were often placed around the outside edge of the room. The rationale for this was that the teacher could easily see all the computer screens and check that students were doing what they ought to be doing. However, as many teachers quickly discovered, this also meant that students would come into the room and sit down with their backs partially or completely to the teacher. Many unhappy minutes have been spent by these teachers encouraging those students to turn around whilst they seek to explain something. Obviously, this is not ideal and, in the worst case scenarios, can lead to all kinds of further problems. Seek to pre-empt these. At some point, have a look at the design of some of the more modern computer laboratory spaces in a school. They look very different from the older design described above. Ask yourself why?

Lesson planning stage five: your classroom resources

As we have discussed throughout this chapter, your teaching and the students' learning does not take place in a vacuum. In addition to the physical classroom environment, the resources that you use within your classroom will have a key impact on the way in which you teach and the way in which your students learn. Resources can include:

- Toys and games
- Books, including exercise books, text books and other reference materials
- Art materials
- Musical instruments
- Computers and other forms of digital technology
- Pieces of software
- Internet resources including music, video or other files
- And anything else you use in your teaching.

Choose your classroom resources wisely

The first and most important piece of advice here is to choose your classroom resources wisely. Use frameworks like Wertsch's mediated action that we explored in the opening of this chapter to help interrogate your own thinking about a particular resource and what it might be able to facilitate within your work. But also be open to the limitations that it might impose. In a previous book that I wrote with my colleague Clive McGoun (Savage and McGoun 2012), we explored how the choice of writing tool impacts on the ways in which students think about words and their writing.

We noticed that word-processing technologies such as those found on many computers, tablets and other mobile devices are pervasive in our schools. The option to produce text on a screen as opposed to by hand is often made uncritically (both by teachers and by students). Picking up on Wertsch's fourth principle of mediated action, we considered some of the historical narratives surrounding the development of these tools. Carr (2010, pp. 17–19) recounts the story of the famous philosopher Nietzsche who, suffering from many ailments that threatened to jeopardise his career as a writer, ordered a typewriter to be delivered to his lodgings in 1882. The Malling-Hansen Writing Ball was an object of great beauty that, with practice, allowed him to write up to 800 characters a minute. It was the fastest typewriter that had been made.

Nietzsche was so delighted with this technology that he composed a short ode to it:

> The writing ball is a thing like me: made of iron
> Yet easily twisted on journeys.
> Patience and tact are required in abundance,
> As well as fine fingers, to use us.

But, as Carr reports, the writing ball began to have a more subtle effect on Nietzsche's work. His friend, the writer and composer Heinrich Köselitz, began to notice changes in his writing style:

> Nietzsche's prose had become tighter, more telegraphic. There was new forcefulness to it, too, as though the machine's power – its 'iron' – was, through some mysterious metaphysical mechanism, being transferred into the words it pressed in the page. (Carr 2010, p. 18)

Köselitz's letter to Nietzsche is fascinating. In his own work, he said, his 'thoughts in music and language often depend on the quality of the pen and paper'. Nietzsche replied, 'You are right, our writing equipment takes part in the forming of our thoughts' (Kittler 1999; Nyíri 1994; Cate 2005).

The story of Nietzsche and his typewriter demonstrates that the tools we choose to use for our writing impose limitations on us as well as opening up possibilities. 'We shape our tools', observed John Culkin, 'and thereafter they shape us' (Culkin 1967, p. 52).

Please do not think that I am suggesting that we should limit students' access to such tools. I would never be as bold and prescriptive as that. These reflections do remind us that we need to think more carefully about the consequences of using such tools. Uncritical choices of tool can lead to many difficulties.

Organise and prepare your classroom resources carefully

Second, and on a much more practical level, be organised. Make sure that all the resources you need for any lesson are listed on your lesson plan. Prior to the lesson commencing, use this list to collect together and check that you have everything ready. There is nothing worse than the flow of the lesson being disrupted because you are having to find something that you thought you had but has just magically disappeared!

In addition to ensuring that you have listed all the resources that you need for a lesson, ensure that they are well prepared. If you are using textbooks, make sure you have enough copies for all the students and you know which page number(s) you are wanting to refer to; if you are using musical or video examples, have these edited to the right portion and/or length to avoid having to fumble through your iTunes library; if you are using a worksheet, have this photocopied clearly and make sure there are enough copies for all the students. These are all very basic points but you would be amazed how many times I watch lessons where either the lack or inappropriate organisation of basic resources leads to a negative impact on the students' learning opportunities.

For resources that are used regularly within your lessons, consider how they are stored within the classroom. In addition to making sure that there are enough calculators or set squares, ask yourself whether they are easily accessible. As a general rule, you will want to keep the movement of students around your classroom to a minimum. So what practical strategies can you adopt to ensure that key resources are made available to students quickly and easily?

Certain subject areas such as art and science are very resource-rich. If you are in the process of initial teacher education and you work in a subject that perhaps uses less resources, why not observe a few lessons in these curriculum areas with the view of learning some lessons to translate into your own teaching. As someone who has worked in secondary schools for most of my career, I would also recommend observing how primary school teachers manage the considerable number of resources that they use in their teaching.

In the final part of this chapter I am going to consider three further very important areas of classroom resources that you will need to consider in your lesson planning. These are:

- Digital technologies

- Classroom displays

- Other adults who may be in your classroom.

Working with digital technologies

The use of digital technologies is probably the fastest area of expansion in relation to this discussion of resources and their use within classrooms. As with any resources, digital technologies can be both an opportunity to develop teaching and learning in positive ways and a hindrance or limitation to teaching and learning when not used in an informed or skilful way.

There are many obvious benefits to the use of digital technologies in education. First, you can use digital tools to facilitate the development of your own pedagogy. You might want to use presentational technologies to help bring to life key concepts or ideas in a dynamic way; you might want to utilise tracking and assessment software to help chart students' development over time; you might want to use recording technologies to help reflect on your own teaching and evaluate areas for further improvement. All this, and much more beside, are easily achievable using current technologies.

Second, you will seek to include digital technologies within the teaching episodes that you are planning. Students might use a scanner to create a framework for their own artwork, a digital recorder to record and reflect on their musical compositions, a piece of design software to experiment with alternative formats for a particular product, or presentational software such as Prezi to prepare a class presentation.

Many teachers are also beginning to use social, collaborative tools to help their students connect together their learning inside and outside the classroom. Examples include the provision of homework tasks through a school network, the sharing of student work within secure social spaces, the use of curriculum content from remote sources around the world, and the provision of feedback on students' work by talented 'experts' from a specific field.

In all these cases, it is important to remember that the processes of teaching and learning with a digital technology is not the same as teaching and learning without it. Many of the technologies I have mentioned above are very powerful and can transform the processes of teaching and learning in helpful ways. But Wertsch's principles of mediated action tell us that this may not always be the case.

As with many schools, at the university where I work the technological pace has picked up quickly in recent years. In the last couple of years, a new Moodle platform has been implemented; iPads have been given to all staff; new members of staff have been appointed to assist staff with what is hoped will be their 'technologically enhanced' teaching; on many courses students themselves are being given iPads for use during their studies; electronic submission of assignments is fast becoming the norm. I could go on.

But for many teachers, the embrace of technology in our professional and private lives is far from ideal and not something that should advance unchecked. Many writers are expressing increasing reservations about the impact of mobile and social technologies and the detrimental effect they play in our lives. This is particularly true in an educational context. Mark Bauerlein's *The Dumbest Generation: How the Digital Age Stupefies Young Americans and Jeopardizes Our Future* (Bauerlein 2008) presents a compelling alternative that we would be wise to consider. In his wonderful blog on this book, Peter Lawler (Lawler 2013) asks the question about whether this might be both the smartest and dumbest generation that has ever existed. Through twelve provocative points, he amplifies Bauerlein's thesis in a highly entertaining way:

1 Virtually all of our students have hours – and often many, many hours – of daily exposure to screens.

2 So they excel at multitasking and interactivity, and they have very strong spatial skills.

3 They also have remarkable visual acuity; they're ready for rushing images and updated information.

4 But these skills don't transfer well to – they don't have much to do with – the non-screen portions of their lives.

5 Their screen experiences, in fact, undermine their taste and capacity for building knowledge and developing their verbal skills.

6 They, for example, hate quiet and being alone. Because they rely so much on screens keeping them connected, they can't rely on themselves. Because they're constantly restless or stimulated, they don't know what it is to enjoy civilized leisure. The best possible punishment for an adolescent today is to make him or her spend an evening alone in his or her room without any screens, devices, or gadgets to divert him or her. It's amazing the extent to which screens have become multidimensional diversions from what we really know about ourselves.

7 Young people today typically are too agitated and impatient to engage in concerted study. Their imaginations are impoverished when they're visually unstimulated. So their *eros* is too. They can't experience anxiety as a prelude to wonder, and they too rarely become seekers and searchers.

8 They have trouble comprehending or being moved by the linear, sequential analysis of texts.

9 So they find it virtually impossible to spend an idle afternoon with a detective story and nothing more.

10 That's why they can be both so mentally agile and culturally ignorant. That's even why they know little to nothing about how to live well with love and death, as well as why their relational lives are so impoverished.

11 And that's why higher education – or liberal education – has to be about giving students experiences that they can't get on screen. That's even why liberal education has to have as little as possible to do with screens.

12 Everywhere and at all times, liberal education is countercultural. And so today it's necessarily somewhat anti-technology, especially anti-screen. That's one

reason among many I'm so hard on MOOCs, online courses, PowerPoint, and anyone who uses the word 'disrupting' without subversive irony.

I like that Lawler highlights, simultaneously, the potential affordances and limitations of screens and the experiences that they present. However, I am also sure that there is much here that you will agree and disagree with. For me, though, point 11 is telling and I agree entirely with him on this. Higher education, liberal education, in fact any education, must be about giving students experiences that they cannot get on screen, not just seek to replicate things on screens in insipid ways.

It seems to me that in the field of digital technologies we need to be very critical about the affordances and limitations that they offer for education. Here, as much as anywhere, using the principles of mediated action can help us gain a more detailed understanding of these powerful tools and the contexts within which we want to use them.

In terms of practical advice, here are a few tips from my experience of working with ICT in various teaching and learning contexts:

- Always work with the technology yourself before using it with your students.

- Resist the temptation to replace or upgrade technologies for the sake of it. Tried and tested ICT is often better than the latest innovation.

- Remember that most pieces of technology are not designed for the educational space. So your pedagogy with any specific technology will need to be skilful and refined in order to get the most out of it.

Finally in this section on digital technologies, why not consider making greater use of the tools that students themselves might be able to bring with them to their lessons? There is one obvious example. The mobile devices that many students have today contain significant amounts of processing power, applications and software that would rival the computers that schools were using just a few years ago. Many schools are beginning to embrace the power of these technologies. In one school I visited recently, the Art teacher was encouraging students to use the cameras on their phones to provide a visual record of their artwork as it developed over the course of a lesson and upload this to their shared folder on the school network. Whilst he did have other digital cameras available, even this basic use of a phone ensured that all students created a digital portfolio of their work and stored this effectively with no work required on his part!

As with any resource, our pedagogy will need to develop in line with the resources such as mobile phones in a more systematic and rigorous way if the educational benefits of such a technology are to be developed in our schools. There will be particular challenges that will exercise you and your school as a whole, but there are many positive opportunities too.

Classroom displays

The provision of classroom displays is an integral part of creating a positive environment for teaching and learning within your classroom. In this sense, they are an important educational resource that need critical thought. In previous eras, teachers would have to invest a considerable amount of their time designing and producing classroom displays, making sure they looked attractive and presentable. Today, you may have support in helping you produce such displays, but the educational role and function of displays is still under your control.

Classroom displays can have a number of functions. They can be used to:

- Celebrate students' achievements in your subject.

- Provide key information about your subject, including subject knowledge or assessment processes.

- Reinforce expectations for work within your subject or wider school environment.

- Stimulate and create student interest in your subject.

- Provide something extra for students to do.

- Communicate what other classes, teachers or other groups from outside the school may be doing.

As with all these resources, there are some key features that you will need to consider:

- Each display should have a teaching or learning focus. They might be linked to a particular unit of work that you are currently teaching or, alternatively, the previous unit of work so that you can remind students about what they have studied already and how this relates to their current studies.

- If the display includes students' work, think carefully about whose work is being displayed, how it is displayed and why.

- Use high-quality display materials where possible, and keep the display well maintained (and protected if necessary). There is nothing worse that a shabby display.

■ Make reference to your classroom displays as part of your regular teaching. Use them to highlight key teaching points, illustrate particular processes or exemplify a particular learning outcome.

This final point is probably the most crucial one to consider as you engage in the process of lesson planning. As I have said throughout this chapter, you need to place the resources that will be at your disposal during the lesson alongside your planning for the learning objectives and learning outcomes and how these will be facilitated through your teaching activities and episodes. Contextualising your plan in this way will help you immensely as you enact your plan through your skilful pedagogy.

In addition to the manufacture of your own classroom displays (which, I would argue, are a very important area of resource), there are also a large number of companies producing classroom display materials. These are of variable quality and you need to be selective about what to include. In reality, a mixture of published and 'home-made' materials is probably most teachers' standard practice. However, I would encourage you to think really seriously about creating your own display materials whenever possible. This is going to have a more positive impact on your students' learning and help you develop a more integrated pedagogy too.

Although the majority of your teaching will take place within classrooms around the school, it is also worth mentioning that there are a range of other locations in school and beyond where display materials can be placed. You may well be asked to provide materials for these alternative venues and this can be a useful way to help promote your subject or your students' work to the broader school or local community. Typical locations for these displays include corridors, staircases, reception areas, school library facilities, the staff room and even other public places in your local community such as the library, health centre and civic spaces. Whilst this might seem like a lot of additional work, when done well it can help raise the profile of your subject and your students' work within it in a very helpful way.

> **REFLECTIVE TASK**
>
> How can the classroom displays that I produce for my classroom help promote active learning? What will they contain, and where will they be positioned, to ensure that they become an integrated part of my pedagogy?

Using other adults in the classroom

So far, we have considered the resource of the physical environment of the classroom itself, as well as the other resources, digital technologies and displays found within it. In this section we are going to turn to another very important resource that you may have at your disposal: other adults.

There are many other adults, apart from teachers, who may be found working in classrooms today. Parents can be a valuable resource, particularly in the primary school it seems. I have noted that parents are often called upon to listen to children read, help with sports activities, play the piano, and provide extra-curricular activities and clubs. In addition to parents, you may also find classroom assistants, EAL (English as an Additional Language) workers, classroom support staff, special needs assistants and others working within your classroom at various times.

If there is another adult in the classroom, then it is your responsibility as the teacher to manage or co-manage their work. This means that you have to think about their role as part of your lesson planning process. When I have talked to teachers about this, there is one common problem that seems to emerge: finding the time to talk with the other adults and prepare them, in advance, for the particular lesson that you are teaching. In schools that manage this process well, teachers know well in advance who they will be working with in their classes week by week. This allows them to plan appropriately and develop a relationship with the other adult, ensuring that, over time, positive routines are established which result in an enhanced opportunity for student learning. If, however, you have other adults coming into your lessons on a sporadic basis, or perhaps they have numerous teachers to liaise with, the opportunity for this detailed level of planning is minimal. This can have negative consequences.

Effective planning is central to the process of maximising the benefit of having another adult in the classroom with you. Key questions that you will need to consider include:

- What do I want the other adult(s) *specifically* to do?

- How can I convey this information to them simply and rapidly, particularly if this other adult is not somebody that I normally work with?

- Do I want them to work with a pupil, a group of students, or to work with a range of learners?

- Where do I want them to be at different times in the lesson?

- Do I need to prepare any specific materials for them?

As we have discussed already, the best practice in the engagement of other adults in your classroom is to have regular planning sessions where your planning for the lesson can be shared and discussed. But in the reality of everyday life, this can be a luxury! Knowing in advance how everyone's time can best be put to good use is helpful. This is part of your role and it needs to be planned for in your lesson planning.

PRACTICAL TASK

Next time you visit a school, ask about the school policy in relation to other adults working within classrooms. Make sure that you are fully aware of the roles and responsibilities for these other adults and how you can work collaboratively with them to help your lessons run effectively.

Homework and outside learning (or learning beyond the classroom)

Finally, and as something of an aside (although it is an important one), I would like to briefly consider alternative sites for teaching and learning (i.e. those that are outside your normal classroom). Outside learning, or learning beyond the classroom, has always been a part of the provision that most schools have offered to their students. In recent years, a number of new strategies have emerged that have proved very useful to teachers wanting to think in a more holistic way about how the teaching and learning that takes place, week by week, within their classroom can be helpfully linked to broader experiences that students may have outside of formal schooling.

At the heart of this approach is an obvious point: students do not stop learning the moment they walk out of your classroom door! As we have seen already, many of the structural systems that schools adopt compartmentalise learning into manageable chunks. In the majority of secondary schools, there are timetabled days with set periods of time for particular activities or lessons; teachers are employed with a specialism in a particular subject; different classrooms are set up for particular types of learning or subjects, and so on. All these can unhelpfully limit our understanding of the broader processes of learning that span beyond the school boundary. Although many of these delineations may not be so strong in primary schools, there are various curricula or activity-based delineations that can limit opportunities for broader learning to emerge.

The most obvious type of learning outside the classroom is, of course, homework. Homework is a feature of the vast majority of students' lives from primary school onwards. Most teachers would say that the key purpose of homework is to raise standards of attainment (although the research evidence for this assertion is, in reality, a little patchy). Generally though, schools seem to consider homework to be a good thing and you will probably be expected to set homework for your students and mark it. So how can you do this well?

First, avoid using homework as an opportunity for students to 'finish off' what they have done, or were meant to have done, in their lesson. As Stern comments, this is unfair and unreasonable:

> They are unfair because they penalise slower workers and reward quicker workers, which usually (though by no means always) penalises the lower

achieving pupils and rewards the higher achieving pupils. They are unreasonable because the pupils (notably the slower-working pupils) are likely to need a teacher's support. (Stern 2009, p. 23)

Vatterott (2014) has some excellent advice. A good homework task, she suggests, should have five main characteristics:

First, the task has a clear academic purpose, such as practice, checking for understanding, or applying knowledge or skills. Second, the task efficiently demonstrates student learning. Third, the task promotes ownership by offering choices and being personally relevant. Fourth, the task instills a sense of competence – the student can successfully complete it without help. Last, the task is aesthetically pleasing – it appears enjoyable and interesting. (Ibid.)

These are helpful suggestions, and translate readily into a number of contexts. As you are planning your lesson plan, you should also be planning the related homework activity with these five characteristics in mind. Do not treat homework as an after-thought. If you do not take it seriously, then it is no surprise if students do not take it seriously either. Good homework extends students' learning, whereas bad homework just breeds their resentment. Make sure that the homework gives students an opportunity to address your learning objective and outcomes in a different way, or at least that it builds on the key learning that you have generated through the lesson that you have taught.

As well as the provision of an integrated and carefully planned homework strategy, there are strong arguments in favour of all students having a regular opportunity to learn outside the classroom as an integral part of their mainstream schooling. The Council for Learning Outside the Classroom believe that:

Learning outside the classroom is about raising young people's achievement through an organised, powerful approach to learning in which direct experience is of prime importance. Meaningful learning occurs through acquiring skills through real life hands-on activities. This is not only about what we learn, but most importantly, how and where we learn. (Council for LOtC 2012)

Drawing on their advice, if you are planning a visit to an external site, there are a number of factors that you will need to think about before taking your students outside your classroom on a school trip:

■ Be imaginative about your choice of outside learning opportunities. Organising a trip to an outside location can be very time consuming and expensive. It is important to have a clear objective for the trip and to be able to justify this in terms of time and money. It is also important to make strong links to the learning objectives within your curriculum planning and show how the trip will extend and enrich these in a productive way.

■ If this is done well, use the opportunity to engage in learning outside the normal classroom environment to help structure the teaching and learning opportunities prior to the trip and after it. Think about the various curriculum links and opportunities that such a trip will facilitate and integrate these in your broader unit of work over the longer term.

■ Consider the various risks involved. Get the support of the member of staff with responsibility for health and safety issues when students are taken outside their normal school environment. There are also various legal responsibilities that you, and other teachers going on the trip, will need to ensure are met.

■ Make sure you know about the 'charging policy' for school trips that your school operates by. You will need to consider how the trip can be costed properly and ensure that all students can access it fairly.

■ Communicate clearly with your students' parents and carers well in advance of the trip itself. You will need their permission and you will want to ensure that they have a full understanding of the purposes for the trip in terms of the curriculum opportunities it offers their child.

In addition to taking your students to locations outside their immediate school environment, do not forget that nearly every school has an outside environment of its own that you can exploit imaginatively. Whilst it may not be as exciting as a trip to a remote location, it would certainly prove to be less demanding in terms of your time and organisation, and less expensive to the school or parents, but equally rewarding.

Summary

This chapter has explored a number of different areas of resource for your lesson planning. We started by examining a framework for the analysis of our actions within particular contexts: mediated action. Drawing on this, we have considered the physical environment of the classroom itself and how this can be utilised to promote teaching and learning. We have also looked at the wider range of resources, both physical and digital, as well as other human resources, all of which can be productively utilised to help you deliver your learning objectives in a supportive and meaningful context. In the previous section, we also considered how thinking about opportunities for students' learning outside the classroom, whether through an integrated approach to homework or visiting external sites, can usefully enhance the learning that takes place within your classroom.

As we close this chapter, I want to briefly consider some of the other forms of resource and support that you could draw on as you develop your teaching career. I am conscious that many readers of this book will either be undertaking a programme of initial teacher education or will be in the early part of their career. It is vital for all of you to build a strong and robust network of support and resource around yourselves. Teaching is a very demanding career. It can also be very isolating. But working collaboratively within a network is key to enjoying a long and productive teaching career. So if you have not done so already, why not:

1   Join a subject association. These exist for the vast majority of subjects being taught in our schools (some have more than one!) and will give you the opportunity to meet up with other teachers who share a passion for your subject in your local area, virtually through chat rooms, and at national events such as annual conferences.

2   Use other online forums to network. There are loads of these. Two of the largest are those run by the *Times Educational Supplement* (www.tes.co.uk/forums.aspx?nav code=14) and *The Guardian* (http://teachers.guardian.co.uk/). Both of these sites allow you to network virtually with teachers across a range of subject or other themed education fora.

3   Utilise LinkedIn, Twitter, Facebook and other social media to help your networking. Whilst these tools might not be for everyone, it is important to recognise that they are playing an increasingly important part in contemporary life.

4   Develop a link to your local higher education institution. Many of these run teacher education programmes, both for initial teacher training and for continuing professional development, and welcome the input of teachers within these programmes. You may also be interested in hosting a student teacher within your department or school. This can have very positive benefits for your work as well as the student.

5   Prioritise making some links to teachers in other local schools. These links used to be developed by local authority education officers but this is seldom the case any more. Local links established by schools as part of broader education networks can help you, as an individual teacher, find out about what is going on in the school down the road and lead to the development of productive networking opportunities at a personal level.

Effective networking has many positive benefits. One danger of teaching is becoming professionally isolated. Be proactive about the establishment of an appropriate network of support for yourself and your work. Draw on some of the resources outlined above and contribute to them too. Not only will this help you teach better but it will also make teaching a more rewarding activity that will sustain your interest and motivation throughout your career.

Further reading

Wertsch, J. V. (1998) *Mind as Action,* Chapter 2. New York and Oxford: Oxford University Press.

Although it is listed in the references for this chapter and I have explored several of the ideas contained in this title within this chapter, I would strongly recommend that you read at least the second chapter for yourselves. Out of all the literature on human interaction and sociocultural theory, this is one of the most readable chapters that will change the way you perceive teaching.

References

Bauerlein, M. (2008) *The Dumbest Generation: How the Digital Age Stupefies Young Americans and Jeopardizes Our Future.* New York: Penguin.

Carr, N. G. (2010) *The Shallows: What the Internet is Doing to our Brains.* New York: W. W. Norton.

Cate, C. (2005) *Friedrich Nietzsche.* Woodstock, NY: Overlook Press.

Council for LOtC (Learning Outside the Classroom) (2012) www.lotc.org.uk/ (accessed 18 July 2013).

Culkin, J. (1967) 'A schoolman's guide to Marshall McLuhan'. *The Saturday Review,* 18 March, pp. 51–3.

Design Council (2005) *Learning Environments Campaign Prospectus: From the Inside Looking Out.* London: Design Council.

JISC (2006) Designing spaces for effective learning: A guide to 21st century learning space design. www.jisc.ac.uk/uploaded_documents/JISClearningspaces.pdf (accessed 5 July 2013).

Kittler, F. A. (1999) *Gramophone, Film, Typewriter.* Stanford, CA: Stanford University Press.

Lawler, P. (2013) Is this both the smartest and the dumbest generation? http://bigthink.com/ rightly-understood/is-this-both-the-smartest-and-dumbest-generation-3 (accessed 10 March 2014).

McGregor, J. (2007) Understanding and managing classroom space. www.teachingexpertise. com/resources/cpd-resource-understanding-and-managing-classroom-space-3324 (accessed 4 July 2013).

Nyíri, J. C. (1994) 'Thinking with a word processor'. In Casati, R. (ed.) *Philosophy and the Cognitive Sciences.* Vienna: Hölder-Pichler-Tempsky.

Rosenbaum, M. (2009) An illustrated history of pole vault. http://trackandfield.about.com/ od/polevault/ss/illuspolevault_2.htm (accessed 30 November 2013).

Savage, J. and McGoun, C. (2012) *Teaching Contemporary Themes in Secondary Education: Technology, Culture and Communication.* London: Routledge.

Stern, J. (2009) *Getting the Buggers to do their Homework.* London: Continuum.

Vatterott, C. (2014) Five hallmarks of good homework. www.ascd.org/publications/educational-leadership/sept10/vol68/num01/Five-Hallmarks-of-Good-Homework.aspx (accessed 20 May 2014).

Wertsch, J. V. (1998) *Mind as Action.* New York and Oxford: Oxford University Press.

5 Assessing students' learning

Introduction

Learning to use a wide range of assessment is a vital skill that every teacher needs to develop. Assessment processes are characterised in different ways and use different labels. Some of the most common include summative assessment, formative assessment, ipsative assessment and other generic terms such as assessment for learning (AfL).

Numerous books, academic journals and papers have been written about each of these assessment 'types' and it is beyond the space that I have in this book to explore each of them in detail. Rather, I would like to be more practical and direct about how a range of approaches to assessment can be included within your lesson plan and utilised within your teaching. Within this chapter, I would like to do three main things:

- Define a range of simple approaches to assessment and how these can be applied within your lesson plan.

- Consider how you can construct a positive environment in your classroom for any assessment device you choose to use.

- Suggest ways that will ensure that assessment is integrated closely within your teaching.

Defining assessment

In opening this chapter, I think it is important to recognise the two approaches to assessment that have been used within education over the last forty years. These two main approaches are summative assessment and formative assessment.

Summative assessment is about the 'summing up' of students' learning. It is routinely conducted through tests or end-of-unit assessments that seek to identify whether or not key learning objectives have been understood or assimilated by students. One of the most common forms of 'summative' assessment in recent years has been the use of 'levels of attainment' drawn, or interpreted, from the National

Curriculum documentation. However, it is important to establish right at the beginning of this chapter that I do not equate, at any point, assessment as being anything to do with attainment levels. I will consider this point further below.

Formative assessment relates to the ways in which teachers seek to understand how students 'form' their understanding related to a particular learning objective. It is an assessment of the process or progress that they are making towards a particular goal. For many teachers, formative assessment is most closely related to 'Assessment for Learning', a phrase that became popular around the beginning of the twenty-first century and still has an important resonance for many teachers today. Within this chapter, this is the type of assessment with which I am principally concerned.

Types of assessment activities

Put simply, there are numerous different types of assessment activities that you could choose to use in any given lesson that you are planning. Table 5.1 outlines some of the key options for you to consider.

Table 5.1 Types of assessment

Type of assessment	Format of assessment	Benefits and evidence
Closed tasks	▪ Multiple choice tests ▪ True/false items ▪ Filling in blanks ▪ Problem-solving	▪ Useful for assessing a large amount of content quickly ▪ Can assess facts or content easily ▪ Takes less time than other methods
Open tasks	▪ Tasks with a range of different answers ▪ Tasks with various forms of engagement or processes to choose from	Useful for assessing: ▪ A particular process or strategy that you want students to explore ▪ The student's ability to interpret or apply information within a context ▪ Reasoning ▪ The ability to communicate ideas in different forms
Performance tasks	▪ Integrative tasks that will result in specific products ▪ Authentic assessment that is situated within specific subject contexts ▪ Extended projects	Useful for assessing: ▪ The student's ability to organise, synthesise and apply key knowledge, skills or understanding ▪ The use of specific resources for particular ends

Table 5.1 Continued

Type of assessment	Format of assessment	Benefits and evidence
Informal assessments	■ Teacher observations ■ Teacher checklists ■ Conversations with students ■ Interviews with students ■ Teacher journal or diary ■ Lesson evaluations	These approaches can have a whole range of benefits, including: ■ Identifying key elements of a learning process that the student has undertaken ■ Illuminating the understanding that a student has developed over time ■ The social and collaborative context of the learning that has resulted in an individual or group of students
Self-assessment, peer-assessment and reflection	■ Student journals or pieces of reflective writing ■ Peer-review mechanisms such as checklists or other forms of extended writing ■ Group (whole class or subdivided smaller group) reflective activities ■ Daily or weekly self-evaluations ■ Teacher–student interviews ■ Peer-group interviews	These approaches can: ■ Develop students' awareness of their strengths and weaknesses ■ Engage students in a conscious and deliberate application of a range of thinking skills ■ Can model to students the procedural and cognitive skills needed to reason and reflect at a high level ■ Reveal students' natural dispositions towards certain topics or favoured approaches to learning ■ Help you, and other students, identify a range of personal goals for a sequence of new learning

(Adapted from Marzano 2006)

PRACTICAL TASK

Consider the various assessment approaches identified in Table 5.1. Which ones are summative in nature? Which ones are formative? Can any be used in either way?

Lesson planning stage six: your assessment strategy

Given such a broad range of assessment types and processes, how do you decide which assessment technique(s) should be included within a specific lesson plan?

My initial response to this really important question is this: choose the assessment technique(s) that will give you the best opportunity of finding out whether students have engaged with and assimilated the learning objective that you have set for the lesson. This is the number one priority. As we discussed in Chapter 2, your learning objective(s) for a lesson, and the learning outcomes that flow from this, need to be carefully constructed in order to give you a clear focus for that lesson. They should pinpoint a precise area of learning in your particular subject or topic for that lesson around which the teaching activities should have been designed. If this has been done carefully and with the appropriate degree of precision, then you should be able to choose a specific assessment tool quite easily which will allow you to document the learning that the students have undertaken in a natural and relatively straightforward way.

As Table 5.1 illustrates, simple forms of assessment might involve closed tasks that allow you to check whether students have learnt basic elements of knowledge as a result of your lesson – for example, the pH values associated with certain chemicals. Other more open-ended forms of assessment may be more suited to them exploring a creative process they have worked through – for example, expressing the disappointment felt by a particular character in a play through a short piece of drama.

My second response to this important question is this: try to vary who is doing the assessment in your lesson. Perhaps you will think this is a curious answer, but it is my firm belief that assessment need not always be done by the teacher. There are two other key ways that assessment can be conducted within the classroom. Both of these involve the students directly themselves. They can assess their own work, and they can assess each other's.

Self-assessment is a particularly powerful tool. In my experience, some students will take to this quite readily whilst others will need to be strongly guided in the early stages to use self-assessment techniques constructively. Like any cognitive activity, the skills involved in learning to assess one's own performance need to be taught and you should not presume that these will just appear by chance in your students' minds! These skills will need to be introduced, sequenced and modelled by yourself in order to become part of the repertoire of assessment approaches that your students can use.

Similarly, peer-assessment techniques can also be very powerful when used in a positive and constructive way. However, used carelessly they can result in negativity between students and this is best avoided. I would suggest you exercise caution and would steer you away from using peer-assessment too often in your classroom. It should certainly not become the default mode of assessment in your pedagogy.

PRACTICAL TASK

Consider the planning you are undertaking for a lesson in the near future. Having defined your learning objectives and outcomes for the lesson, think about the various assessment types or strategies in Table 5.1 and how they may, or may not, help you gain an understanding of your students' learning in that lesson. Choose the assessment type that you think will give you the greatest degree of insight into your students' learning and write a short statement of between 40 and 60 words that outlines your assessment approach for the lesson.

Beware! Levels of attainment

Assessment, whether done by you or your students, is firmly embedded within your pedagogy and is integral to your lesson plan. Done skilfully, it can really help you gain a full understanding of how the students in your class have understood the learning objective(s) that you have set for your lesson.

However, in recent years an approach to assessment built around levels of attainment has dominated the English school education system. In order to understand how this situation emerged, a short historical detour is required.

The first National Curriculum was implemented in 1992. This legal framework for the education of children between the ages of 5 and 16 was debated and discussed by politicians and educationalists for several years prior to this date. As part of the provision, each subject had a number of attainment targets. These attainment targets were paragraphs of text that described the learning that students had to achieve at certain age levels (7, 11, 14 and 16).

In the first revision of the National Curriculum in 2000, this system was expanded by the adoption of levels of attainment (normally levels one to eight, with an exceptional level in some subjects). These levels described in detail the progress that students might make as they worked towards the attainment target(s) described in the National Curriculum. However, and this is really important, the levels of attainment were only meant to be used once at the end of each key stage (i.e. when students reached the age of 7, 11 and 14; at 16 students would be assessed by the GCSE examination). In other words, levels of attainment should have been used as a summative assessment tool (as a way of 'summing up' students' learning at key points).

Sadly, schools did not use levels of attainment in this way. They began to create database- and spreadsheet-driven systems of assessment that used these summative levels of attainment in what can best be described as a formative way (i.e. as a process of helping them to form judgements about a student's progress). Many of the following approaches were common throughout the first part of the twenty-first century (and many of these you will still see in place in schools today):

1 Schools created sublevels for student attainment. This could involve the addition of a letter such as h (higher), m (middle) and l (lower) to the numerical level, resulting in eight main levels each subdivided into three intermediate levels (5h, 5m, 5l and so on). In one school I visited recently, there were ten sublevels for each main level.

2 Teachers became required to provide a level, or sublevel, for each student at various points of the academic year (e.g. once every half-term).

3 This resulted in students being monitored or tracked across the year, with reports to parents indicating how much of a level, or sublevel, their child has managed to progress.

4 In order to do this within their subject areas, teachers had to devise a range of approaches to the management of levels in their classrooms. This included structured wall charts to illustrate how progression can be achieved from one sublevel to the next; it has also included the adoption of assessment worksheets or booklets that indicate how students can work towards higher levels in specific tasks.

5 Worst of all, it resulted in teachers awarding individual sublevel marks for individual pieces of work that a student completes. In other words, what was designed as a summative form of assessment became a formative one.

This sorry story of mismanaged and ill-conceived assessment has resulted in a very poor and impoverished model of teaching and learning in our schools. It is overly bureaucratic, it diminishes the value of many other kinds of enriching assessment processes, it is baffling for parents, and it is demeaning to our students who become overly preoccupied with what 'level' they might be working at to the detriment of any other positive formal feedback.

For all these reasons, and many more that I do not have the time or space to discuss here, the current Government in the United Kingdom has *abolished* the levels of attainment in the new National Curriculum that is to be implemented in schools from September 2014. It does not appear in any of the Programmes of Study for any of the subjects. There is *no requirement* on schools to use such a framework of assessment any more. It is my sincere hope that the data-driven, simplistic and tick-box approach to levels and sublevels, as evidenced in the work of many schools, is quickly discarded as new systems are introduced.

In reality of course, this may not happen quickly as schools seem welded to these types of approaches. This is normally because they think it is what Ofsted wants them to do. But this will change over time. I would encourage you not to reduce the value of assessment, and the value of your students' work, through the use of levels of attainment as a formative tool. There are so many better ways that you can conduct assessment as an integrated part of your lesson planning.

Lesson planning stage seven: construct a positive classroom environment

In the above discussion, I have highlighted the two key ways in which teachers have used assessment in their classrooms over the last few years. Whatever assessment device or technique you choose to use (and there are loads to choose from), it is vital that you use this in a constructive way in your teaching. I have emphasised that the formative use of summative tools will also result in a poor assessment strategy.

Whatever assessment process or assessment type you choose to use within a lesson, it will be vital that you create a positive classroom environment for assessment. This will have a direct impact on students' chances of learning successfully. For me, a positive classroom environment means that you must consider the physical, the emotional (or affective) and perceptual (especially pupils' self-efficacy) dimensions of your classroom environment. These will all impinge on the creation of a positive assessment atmosphere.

The physical environment

First, as we saw in the previous chapter, the classroom's physical environment needs to be considered. This will have an effect on a number of factors, some of which are within your control and some of which you will not be able to control. But you should be aware of them all. Here is a list of some of the most common physical environmental features that will all impact on your teaching and your students' learning:

- Seating: the quality of seating and the arrangement of seats around the room.

- Desks: their arrangement. Are they necessary?

- Combination of seating and desks with larger open spaces. Have a look at a range of primary school classrooms to see how the relationship between furniture and open spaces can be maximised for learning.

- Storage: where do pupils store their belongings (books, bags, other personal effects and so on)? Are they accessible? Do they need to be?

- The visual environment through displays of work, posters and other resources.

- The quality of lighting in the room. How many times have you been distracted by that flickering light bulb or the annoying hum that it generates?

- The air quality and temperature. You might not have much control over either of these, but personal preferences for heat or fresh air may not correspond with that of your pupils.

- The provision and location of other resources, including books, items of other equipment, ICT and so on. Issues of where these are positioned and how accessible they are will have an effect on their use and integration within the classroom. We examined this issue at length in the previous chapter.

PRACTICAL TASK

What are the physical aspects of a classroom environment that generate an atmosphere for learning? Spend some time analysing the physical environment of a classroom that you have to teach in regularly. Identify some of the positive and negative physical environmental elements. Start with the list above but there are probably others that you can identify too. What are the consequences of these physical arrangements on the process of teaching and learning? In particular, what effect might they have on processes of assessment?

The emotional and affective environment

Equally important to the construction of a good physical environment for teaching and learning is the construction of a positive affective domain that positively influences students' emotions including their mental disposition, their level of interest and their self-motivation. Perhaps this is more difficult to achieve as it goes beyond the physical dimension (although this is important) and begins to impact on what we do as teachers and gets to the heart of teaching being built upon human relationships. This is especially the case when we focus on assessment, which is often something that students perceive as being done to them rather than being done with them.

Goleman describes pupils' intellectual capacity as working 'in concert' with their emotion (Goleman 1998). You can begin to see this in evidence when you note students' emotional responses to an assessment process. Perhaps they become anxious or frustrated; maybe they show disappointment or embarrassment, pleasure or exhilaration. Either way, or perhaps every way, we can see that students' emotional responses to learning are important facets that need careful handling. Chapman and King (2005, p. 20) take a range of Goleman's identified emotional intelligences and characterise these for assessment activity in the classroom. To these, I have added a number of questions for you to consider as you begin to think through how assessment should work in your classroom.

Self-awareness

Self-awareness involves how a student:

1. Understands feelings

2. Knows his or her strengths and needs

3. Possesses self-confidence.

So, for your chosen assessment process:

1. To what extent does it build up an individual student's self-awareness and self-confidence?

2. How closely can you monitor an individual pupil's emotional response to it and seek to understand their individual perception of it at an emotional level?

Self-regulation

Self-regulation:

1. Delays gratification to pursue goals

2. Works to complete personal and academic tasks

3. Possesses the ability to recover from set-backs.

In relation to your chosen assessment process:

- To what extent does assessment empower individual students to make their own choices about what matters or counts in a particular teaching episode?

- How does it allow students the opportunity to fail, readjust or recover and make further progress?

Motivation

When a student has motivation, they:

1. Show initiative

2. Have an innate desire to improve

3. Keep trying after failure.

So for your assessment process consider:

- Do they give pupils an opportunity to keep trying and build on their natural desire to improve?

- Does the timing of the assessment build a natural sense of pupil motivation through a particular task or series of tasks?

Empathy

We demonstrate empathy when we:

1. Feel what others are feeling

2. Respect diverse views of other individuals

3. Are loyal and supportive.

So for teaching:

- How can we remain sensitive and empathetic to individual students throughout the application of an assessment process?

- In what ways can we model appropriate responses, communicate sensitively and share emotional feelings with our students in response to the outcomes of assessment processes?

Social skills

Social skills are demonstrated in many ways, in particular by:

1. Being a vital team member

2. Communicating effectively through verbal and non-verbal communication

3. Getting along with others

4. Learning during individual, paired and group work.

In relation to your choice of assessment process:

- Have you got a range of assessment strategies in place that emphasise the importance of social skills? Do your students know that on occasions the assessment may be not only about their individual effort and attainment but also about their ability to work constructively with others?

- Have you developed a range of teaching activities that allow for the full range of interactions between students through individual study, paired work and group work?

- How can whole class teaching contain and promote these social processes and how can you assess them in a meaningful and personalised way for each student?

Developing the 'perceptual' environment in assessment

How students perceive their learning is going is a vital element that you will need to consider as you begin to assess their work. This relates directly to the notion of self-efficacy. Self-efficacy is:

> An impression that one is capable of performing in a certain manner or attaining certain goals. It is a belief that one has the capabilities to execute the courses of actions required to manage prospective situations. Unlike efficacy, which is the power to produce an effect (in essence, competence), self-efficacy is the belief (whether or not accurate) that one has the power to produce that effect. (Ormrod 2006)

Although self-efficacy is closely linked to self-esteem (that we discussed above), it is a distinct concept. At a basic level, self-esteem relates to a person's sense of self-worth; self-efficacy relates to a person's perception of their ability to reach a goal. As an example, let us consider my lack of ability to play darts. If, at this moment, I am a terrible darts player, it is quite likely that I have a poor self-efficacy in regard to my ability to play darts. I have no, or very little, belief in my own power to become a better darts player. But, to be honest, this does not affect my own sense of self-esteem very much. I am not that bothered about not being able to play darts.

Thinking about this in an educational context, Bandura (1997) points to four sources that affect self-efficacy. I will use these to make some important points for our consideration of how to create a positive classroom environment for assessment.

Mastery experience

The role of a 'mastery experience' is the most important factor in developing a student's self-efficacy. Simply put, success raises self-efficacy and failure lowers it. Bandura makes the point that we are not easily fooled by empty praise and condescension. Whilst artificial bolstering of our self-esteem is often what is offered in many learning experiences, real strength and the construction of a positive sense of identity and self-efficacy is only achieved by wholehearted and consistent recognition of real accomplishment, that is, achievement that has meaning in the students' culture.

As teachers, it will be vital that you take every opportunity to build up your students' self-efficacy through the use of praise and positive reinforcement. But praise for the sake of praise will not work. In fact, according to Bandura, this will have a negative effect and students will see right through it for what it is. But genuine, authentic praise and encouragement for your students' efforts, done systematically and regularly, will build up their sense of self-efficacy and make your classroom environment a positive one in which success and achievement is valued.

Vicarious experience

Vicarious experiences occur when you see someone like yourself succeeding at something. It is a process of comparison. When you see someone succeeding at something, your self-efficacy will increase; and when you see someone failing, your sense of self-efficacy will decrease. So if a student can see someone like them doing something successfully, the feeling that they can do it too will be enhanced. This process is more effectual when a student can see himself or herself as similar to the person providing the model. Watching Robin van Persie score goals for Manchester United will only achieve so much in terms of self-efficacy! Most of us will never be able to succeed in football at that level. If a student watches another student who they perceive as having similar ability succeed, this will increase their own self-efficacy.

The use of modelling on the provision of vicarious experiences has clear applications for your classroom setting. You can carefully involve students in practical tasks, demonstrations or presentations. Done well, these can have a very positive influence on those watching and result in a boost in their self-efficacy.

Social persuasion

The concept of Bandura's social persuasion relates to conversations we might have and the encouragement or discouragement contained therein. These can have a strong influence on one's sense of confidence and self-efficacy. Conversations with students are a crucial part of any skilful process of assessment in the classroom. You will need to build up in your students an appropriate sense of achievement and pride in their work if their self-efficacy is to increase. Similarly, you will need to teach your students (and remind them regularly) of the power of words when giving feedback to each other in peer-assessment exercises. In terms of self-assessment, you will need to encourage them to be honest in their own feedback on their work, and neither be too harsh nor too celebratory without undue cause.

Physiological factors

Finally, in unusual and stressful situations, most people will exhibit signs of distress such as the shakes, aches and pains, fatigue, fear, nausea and so on. A person's perceptions of these responses can markedly alter their sense of self-efficacy. Bandura gives us a very relevant example. If you get 'butterflies in your stomach' before teaching a lesson and you have low self-efficacy, you may take this as a sign of your own inability. The consequent effect will be a further decrease in your self-efficacy. In contrast, if you have a higher level of self-efficacy, it is likely that you will interpret such physiological signs as normal and unrelated to your actual teaching ability, which you will continue to see as high. It is your belief about the implications of the physiological response that will alter your self-efficacy rather than the power of the response itself.

This may be the most difficult area of self-efficacy to deal with in the classroom. It has a particular relevance to those areas of the curriculum such as music, sport or drama where there are obvious performance elements. In these areas of the curriculum, students will need to be taught that feelings of nervousness or distress can be a natural reaction to stressful situations such as an assessment or perform-ance occasion. A positive channelling or understanding of the physiological response is possible for most students but it will take time to develop and this will need practice.

More generally, all of us need to frame assessment items carefully and monitor our students' responses. This can only be helped by making assessment a natural part of the classroom routine (the key focus of strategies such as assessment for learning) rather than high-profile, one-off occasions where passing an examination becomes an imperative.

REFLECTIVE TASK

How can these key principles about the affective and perceptual domains of assessment be handled carefully within your teaching? How can you ensure in the delivery of a particular assessment strategy that these important considerations are imbued within your pedagogy?

Integrating assessment within your teaching

Assessment is a key part of your pedagogy. It is integral to your teaching. As we will discuss further in Chapter 8, all elements of the lesson planning process, and the choices that you make within that process, will have consequences for how you operate in the classroom. A routine of assessment for learning will also help you form a productive reflective cycle. It will not only give you the information you need about your students' learning, but it will also provide you with useful insights about the effectiveness of your teaching. The assessment of your students and the development of effective teaching are a symbiotic process. They rely upon each other and can usefully inform each other with positive consequences for you and your students.

In the concluding part of this chapter I will explore how the integration between assessment and planning, teaching and reflective practice works in a little more detail. In order to do this, I would like to revisit a piece of foundational research in the area of assessment for learning. *Inside the Black Box* (Black and Wiliam 1998) identified five simple principles that can help you improve your students' learning through assessment. These were:

1 Provide effective feedback to students.

2 Actively involve your students in their own learning.

3 Adjust your teaching to take account of the results of assessment.

4 Recognise the profound influence assessment has on the motivation and self-esteem of pupils, both of which are crucial to learning.

5 Consider the need for students to be able to assess themselves and to understand how to improve.

But there are risks that the report identified in respect of how assessment could be implemented in the classroom. Without careful thought, it is possible that teachers could:

▓ Value quantity and presentation rather than the quality of pupils' learning.

▓ Lower the self-esteem of pupils by over-concentrating on judgements rather than advice for improvement.

▓ Demoralise pupils by comparing them negatively and repeatedly with more successful learners.

▓ Give feedback which serves social and managerial purposes rather than helping pupils to learn more effectively.

▓ Work with an insufficient picture of pupils' learning needs.

In the conclusion of the report, *Inside the Black Box* drew a number of conclusions about what characterises good assessment for learning. The authors stated that successful assessment for learning:

▓ Is embedded in a view of teaching and learning of which it is an essential part.

▓ Involves sharing learning goals with pupils.

▓ Aims to help pupils to know and to recognise the standards they are aiming for.

▓ Involves pupils in self-assessment.

▓ Provides feedback which leads to pupils recognising their next steps and how to take them.

▓ Involves both the teacher and the pupils reviewing, and reflecting on, assessment information.

In my inclusion of key themes from the report, I hope that you will notice my theme of assessment as an integrated part of teaching and learning is richly illustrated! To close, we will explore how this works practically for each of our three examples: planning, teaching activities and review/evaluation.

Assessment as an integrated part of planning

Please ensure that you have assessment in mind from the very first point of your planning for an individual lesson. Whatever assessment strategy you are going to use – formative, summative, peer- or self-assessment – ensure that your lesson plan provides you with opportunity for some kind of assessment activity however simple or routine. Target your assessment process or type on the learning objective(s) that you have set for that lesson. Ensure that you can answer the key question that I stated earlier in this chapter: how will the assessment process or type that you have chosen give you the best opportunity of finding out whether students have engaged with and assimilated the learning objective that you have set for the lesson? Summarise your assessment strategy for the lesson in a short statement of between 40 and 60 words.

Use your lesson plan as a space to frame the opportunities for assessment with your students. How will the students know what the learning objective for the lesson is? Do they need to know? How will they know that they have achieved what you planned? What are the markers or indicators of success that you are expecting to see? At the early stage of a lesson, these things can be communicated simply and quickly.

Finally, you will need to ensure that the assessment approaches that you have planned in respect of learning objectives and outcomes are differentiated and personalised for each student. We will be considering this further in the next chapter. Generally though, students will respond as individuals to the work you have planned. Your assessment practice should build in a process of individual target-setting for each student.

Assessment as an integrated part of teaching

Good teaching is based around a human interaction between the teacher and the student. At its heart, teaching is like a relationship that needs to be initiated, developed, nurtured and valued in order for it to be successful. The assessment of students' work can be done in a caring, sympathetic and empathetic way. It can be done with a culture of shared discovery through which the flow of learning is maintained and enhanced. I would encourage you not to view assessment as something that you 'do' to students. Rather, build in a range of approaches to assessment in your work that make assessment a shared responsibility.

In all the discussion about data, bench-marking, target-setting and the like that you will hear when you go into any school, do not forget that at the heart of teaching are children. These children are real! They are not numbers on a spreadsheet. They come into your classroom with the full range of life's rich tapestry embroidered in their minds. You need to engage with them. You need to understand why they might be feeling the way they are about their work. Blunt objectives, meaninglessly undifferentiated targets and an over-reliance on summative testing will not help them learn better. So, prioritise the development of your own rich pedagogy. Consider and experiment with a large range of assessment processes but always in the light of the key issues that we have discussed in the heart of this chapter. Always keep in your mind the broader affective and perceptual domains that we have discussed above.

As I have suggested throughout this chapter, the outcomes of any assessment process that you undertake in your teaching need to feed forwards into your planning for the next lesson with that class. This is another reason why it is not appropriate for secondary school teachers to use the same lesson plan for every class even if they are studying the same unit of work. I would also urge you to adapt and amend your lesson plans as a unit of work progresses, ensuring that the results of the assessment process proactively shape the focus of learning objectives and outcomes, and the choice of teaching activities, week by week.

Assessment as an integrated part of reflection and evaluation

Third, and perhaps most obviously, assessment has a very important role to play in forming strategies of reflection and evaluation for your lessons. This has a number of dimensions that relate to your own development as a teacher and these will be explored in further detail in Chapter 9.

For our students' benefit, let us note that the reflective feedback that we give to them as part of a process of assessment will be vital in helping them recognise what they have achieved, what their next learning steps will be and how they should take them (some teachers call this 'feed-forward' but I am not that enamoured with that term). The research literature clearly shows that students value oral as well as written feedback on their work. This feedback should take place at different stages within a lesson and be given to individuals and to groups of pupils. Make sure that you plan for this! Feedback should be positive and constructive but not patronising. As we have seen, praise for the sake of praise can have a detrimental effect. But feedback does need to be grounded in reality, in what the student has achieved (however small that might be in some cases) and authentic in its expression. The identification and positive reinforcement of small learning steps enables students to see that they are making progress and over time this will build their sense of self-esteem and self-efficacy.

Involving students in the review and evaluation of the assessment process will generally have a positive impact on their perception of what assessment is for. Shared ownership of the assessment data that you collect can also be a good thing. It demystifies assessment and results in students sharing your model of assessment as an integrated part of the teaching and learning process. However, please remember that this need not always be necessary or desirable. As with all these things, you, as the teacher, need to make decisions based on your professional knowledge and understanding of a particular context.

Summary

In this chapter we have explored how varying types of assessment can impact on the teaching and learning that you are going to undertake. I have argued that the precise type or form of assessment for any one lesson that you teach must relate closely to the learning objective(s) that you have set for that lesson. The assessment process must result in you gaining a greater degree of understanding of your students' learning at the end of the lesson than you had at the start. I have also emphasised that the classroom atmosphere you generate will have a direct impact on your students' chances of learning successfully. You need to take care of your classroom's physical environment, ensuring that it promotes the learning atmosphere you want to develop. But, most importantly, you need to construct a positive affective domain that will enhance pupils' emotional response to learning and develop their emotional intelligence. Generating your students' self-esteem and self-efficacy are also keys to creating a positive classroom atmosphere for assessment. Finally, assessment, teaching and reflection are integrated processes that usefully inform each other and, when conceptualised as such, result in a unified model of teaching in which teachers and students can work together for common ends.

Further reading

Torrance, H. (2011) 'Using assessment to drive the reform of schooling: Time to stop pursuing the chimera?' *British Journal of Educational Studies*, 59:4, 459–485.

The careless imposition of rigid assessment frameworks and their antithetical effect on the opportunity for students to experience authentic educational encounters have been explored by many researchers. I would strongly recommend you start with the work of Professor Torrance. This article presents a challenging call for us to 'stimulate new visions of what might be accomplished by our educational system, and new ways to record diverse experiences and outcomes, rather than continuing to insist that all we can achieve is compliance with that which is already known' (Torrance 2011, p. 482).

References

Bandura, R. (1997) *Self-Efficacy: The Exercise of Control*. New York: W. H. Freeman.

Black, P. and Wiliam, D. (1998) *Inside the Black Box: Raising Standards Through Classroom Assessment*. London: Kings College.

Chapman, C. and King, R. (2005) *Differentiated Assessment Strategies: One Tool Doesn't Fit All*. Thousand Oaks, CA: Corwin Press.

Goleman, D. (1998) *Working with Emotional Intelligence*. New York: Bantam Books.

Marzano, R. J. (2006) *Classroom Assessment & Grading That Work*. Alexandria, VA: Association for Supervision and Curriculum Development.

Ormrod, J. E. (2006) *Educational Psychology: Developing Learners* (5th edition). Upper Saddle River, NJ: J. Merrill. Companion website: http://wps.prenhall.com/chet_ormrod_edpsych_5/0,5159,1774689-,00.html (accessed 18 June 2007).

6 Differentiation and personalisation

Introduction

This chapter opens with a short discussion about you and your identity as a teacher. Understanding yourself is crucial if you are to meaningfully understand others. Each teacher is different and we need to acknowledge and recognise our own sense of identity and build from there as we address the needs of our individual students. Following that, we will examine a number of common whole school strategies for addressing the educational needs of students, before turning our attention to your own individual planning and pedagogy as we look at strategies for personalisation and differentiation within your own classroom.

Every teacher matters

> Good teaching cannot be reduced to technique; good teaching comes from the identity and integrity of the teacher. (Palmer 2009)

Teaching is a distinctly personal thing. As you may have discovered already, watching other teachers work raises as many questions as it does provide answers. Perhaps you have watched an individual teacher manage a group of boisterous students particularly effectively, yet when you tried to adopt a similar behaviour management technique in your own teaching a few days later, it did not have the desired effect. Why was that? Part of the answer is that teaching, at its most basic level, is a human activity that draws on our relationships with other human beings in a fundamental way. These relationships are hard to categorise and define. But one thing is for sure. They take a while to establish and they are informed by our own sense of identity, and how that identity is presented and communicated to others.

For these reasons, this chapter about ensuring that your teaching meets the educational needs of all your students is starting with a brief reflection on you and your sense of identity. I believe that it is almost impossible to understand the needs of others, your students, unless you have a clear understanding of yourself as a teacher, and where your sense of teacher identity has come from.

My dictionary defines 'identity' as:

- The collective aspect of the set of characteristics by which a thing is definitively recognisable or known.

- The set of behavioural or personal characteristics by which an individual is recognisable as a member of a group.

- The quality or condition of being the same as something else.

- The distinct personality of an individual regarded as a persisting entity; individuality.

Identity is about something being known or recognised. For our discussion, it is what makes you the person you are (physically, emotionally, intellectually, spiritually and so on). It may also be elements or characteristics that other people can recognise in you. Second, identity is linked to a relationship. Your identity relates to others that you meet. The particular aspects of your own identity are best understood when you contextualise them in different ways (e.g. your actions in a particular context could be seen as being representative or demonstrative of a specific element of your identity, which can be perceived by others and, therefore, mark you out as a particular individual). This is particularly important when you seek to develop a new identity for a new type of activity (e.g. teaching).

> **REFLECTIVE TASK**
>
> To what extent do you need to establish a new identity to be an effective teacher? Won't you just draw on your existing identity? How much of 'you' actually goes into the 'teacher you'?

As you begin teaching, your existing pre-teaching identity will be challenged and tested in various ways. As we have said already, teaching is a human activity (you have to do it!) and the intellectual, practical, physical and emotional challenges that it contains will take their toll on you as an individual. When I started teaching in my mid-twenties, I remember coming home after a full day at school and often collapsing on the sofa for a short nap. I was physically and intellectually tired. However, the point is that starting to teach really does challenge you as a whole person. It is not a job that you can easily leave behind at the school gate. Many teachers find it hard to switch off and therein lies a whole number of potential problems that we do not have time to explore within this book. But do beware that many teachers leave the profession each year as a result of stress.

It is important to find time in the early days of your teaching career to reflect on this transition from your pre-teaching life to your new role as a teacher. As your teacher identity develops, there will be common elements that you will recognise and find familiar. Elements drawn from your genetic makeup, your up-bringing, your relationships and broader life experiences will all help form part of your teacher identity because they are an integral part of who you are; however, you will find these being augmented with new elements that are drawn from unusual sources including, but not limited to, your memories of teachers who have taught you, other teachers (e.g. your mentors) who you consider to be good role models, and perhaps your peers who you are learning to teach alongside. If you are doing teaching properly, it will be both physically and psychologically demanding, especially as you undergo your initial teacher education and during the first few years of your career.

Therefore, in this chapter that is considering how we can provide for the individual needs of our students, do not forget that you are also an individual! Your teaching identity will be a unique mix of influences and as you seek to understand these for yourself, you will be able to draw on them to help inform your planning and pedagogy. This is one reason why it is so important to undertake the processes of planning and preparation for your own lessons and not take the shortcut of just teaching from someone else's lesson plan. This is seldom, or ever, a good approach. Do you remember the ten questions that opened this book? The answer to question 6 is very relevant here. Make it one of your golden rules never to teach a lesson using someone else's lesson plan. Working hard at providing appropriate strategies for personalisation and differentiation in your lessons will, as I will discuss below, have to be framed by your relationship with the students you teach. Teaching does not occur in a vacuum. Many of the students that you will teach will have challenging individual educational needs that you will need to address. The only way to address these meaningfully is from a position of security about your own identity as a teacher and reaching out to others, our students, from this position of strength.

REFLECTIVE TASK

What are the key strengths in my personality that you can build on to become an effective teacher? Without being too harsh on yourself, what are the areas that you know you need to strengthen? When considering the work of other teachers, what are the key attributes of their personalities and teaching identities that you would like to foster and develop in your own teaching?

School structures

As we have discussed above, your teaching within your classroom does not take place in a vacuum. Understanding your own identity as a teacher and how this informs the ways that you think and act is an important contextualising factor in your work. At a more mundane level, perhaps, are the structures of the school that you are working within. These provide a whole range of influences on your work, not least when it comes to how individual classes of students are formed and various re-combinations of groups of students within specific curriculum areas. There is one key principle that the vast majority of schools abide by when creating these class groups: they keep students of similar ages together.

The influence of the year group

Year groups are the most common structure used by schools through which students are separated in manageable numbers. The 'year' in 'year groups' normally refers to academic years which, for historical reasons, begin on 1 September. Within most areas of the country, all pupils whose birthday falls between the beginning of September of one year and the end of August in the following year become a 'year group'.

This organisational principle is seldom questioned by the general public despite there being a broad range of educational research showing that it has a detrimental effect on students' academic development, particularly those who are born towards the end of each academic year (those children with birthdays in June, July or August). Research done by the Institute for Fiscal Studies and the Nuffield Foundation in 2011 (Crawford et al. 2011) revealed that not only did babies born in the autumn term do better in their education (as measured by a statistical analysis of their examination results) than those babies born in the summer term but, in addition to this general trend, also the month of a child's birth was a major influence on their skill development. Their key findings state that:

> In line with previous literature, we find evidence of large and significant differences between August- and September-born children in terms of their cognitive skills, whether measured using national achievement tests or alternative indicators such as the British Ability Scales. These gaps are particularly pronounced when considering teacher reports of their performance; moreover, they are also present when considering differences in socio-emotional development and engagement in a range of risky behaviours. The absolute magnitude of these differences decreases as children get older, suggesting that August-borns are 'catching up' with their September-born peers in a variety of ways as the difference in relative age becomes smaller over time. (Ibid., p. 2)

Research done by Cambridge Associates confirms these findings, noting that the effects are most severely felt within the primary school:

> The birthdate effect is most pronounced during infant and primary school but the magnitude of the effect gradually and continually decreases through Key Stage 3, 4, and A level . . . The disadvantage for August-born children over September-born children in expected attainment dropped from an average of 25% at KS 1 to 12% at KS 2, to 9% at KS 3, to 6% at KS 4 and to 1% at A level.

Despite this decrease, the effect remains significant at GCSE, A level and in respect of entry into higher education. (Skyes et al. 2009, p. 3)

Given research like this, it is curious that the system of dividing year groups by student age has not been challenged more rigorously either by policy-makers or parents. But even in today's educational climate with schools enjoying a greater degree of autonomy than ever before, there are few schools that are re-engineering the year group approach and managing their groups of students in different ways. One obvious way might be to create mixed-ability streams of students that cross age-related boundaries. At first sight this might seem sensible, but there is clear research by the OECD that this is ineffective (Field et al. 2007, p. 78).

Interestingly, I was discussing this point with someone whilst watching my son play rugby. We were talking about the disparity in height and weight between the boys (all aged between 12 and 13 years old). Within some teams, this is having a major influence on the coaching strategies being employed. Whilst every coach wants their team to win, to do so by just giving the ball to the largest player and telling him to run his way through the opposition is clearly only going to have limited value longer term. Individual flair or dominance is one thing, but teamwork is much more important in the long run. By the time the boys reach the ages of 16 to 17, many of their physical differences will have evened out substantially. In other parts of the world, particularly in Australia and New Zealand, school-boy rugby is organised according to the height and weight of the boys, and not by their age. This has had a very large impact on the style of coaching that is being adopted in these countries and, apparently, it is something that the Rugby Football Union here in the United Kingdom is looking at in some detail.

It seems that the organisation of students into academic year groups is done principally for organisational benefits rather than educational ones. I find it hard to imagine this situation changing at any point soon. For this reason, you will need to be pragmatic in your work. Do find out when your students' birthdays are, in recognition that they are a major indicator of potential academic and other performance success (especially in the primary school). Whilst not every child born in August is going to suffer educationally (just like every child born in September is not going to succeed), being aware of these issues and watching out for those younger students in your classes who need additional, targeted support should become an important part of your planning and preparation.

I am not suggesting that schools should group their students in different ways. However, as a teacher, it is important to recognise that these structural approaches are not value-neutral and they will impact on the ways in which you plan for teaching and learning to take place.

Within these year group structures, students are organised within classes. At this point there are two broad strategies that dominate the majority of schools: mixed-ability classes or those differentiated by ability (streaming and setting). As Ireson and Hallam comment, each strategy has its own perceived benefits:

There do, however, appear to be differential benefits for students in selective and unselective systems. Selection and ability grouping tend to work to the advantage of students in the higher attaining groups, while unselective systems and mixed ability grouping tend to benefit those in the lower attaining groups. (Ireson and Hallam 2001, p. 17)

It will be important that you give some thought to the particular impact of your teaching within both types of grouping.

Mixed-ability classes

For many teachers in primary and secondary schools, students will be taught in mixed-ability classes differentiated by age group. Philosophically, I think that any teacher faced with a class with more than one student in a class is teaching a mixed-ability class! But, more generally, 'mixed ability' means that students of all abilities will be present within the class. This will include students who are 'gifted and talented' as well as those who may have been recognised as having acute special educational needs.

For primary school teachers, mixed-ability classes are the norm. If you are working within this context, you will be working mainly with the same group of students each day. This allows you to form very strong relationships with individual students and really get to know their particular strengths and weaknesses well. This has a tremendous advantage when it comes to planning work and devising strategies for personalisation and differentiation. Working in a secondary school setting is very different. Here, you are likely to see anywhere between 200 and 300 different students every week. You will also be spending less time with each student. This makes the task of creating specific strategies for personalisation and differentiation much more difficult.

Within the field of educational research, teachers' perceptions of mixed-ability classes has been studied in some detail. Whilst it is not the purpose of this chapter to argue for the teaching of students in mixed-ability classes throughout the school, it is interesting to read that teachers do respond differently when they are teaching a class with a particular grouping. For example, Ireson and Hallam comment that:

The great majority of teachers teaching sets expected a faster rate of work from the more able students (89%). In mixed ability classes there was less expectation that able students would work at a faster rate (69%). Whether students were in mixed ability or set classes, the majority of teachers expected greater depth of work from the more able students (86%). In mixed ability classes teachers expected more independent thought from the higher ability students (84%) than in set classes (76%). Most teachers expected the more able children to take greater responsibility for their own written work whether they were in mixed ability (71%) or sets (76%). (Ibid., p. 139)

Sets and streams

Within common educational parlance, setting is when students are 'set' for their ability within a specific subject area – for example, Mathematics. In this model, an individual student might be in one set for Mathematics, but may be in a different set entirely for English. Streaming is slightly different. In this model, students are put into groups through some general testing of ability or aptitude and then taught in these groups across the curriculum.

At I mentioned above, regardless of age, school or grouping, any teacher who teaches more than one student at a time is teaching in a mixed-ability environment. It is important to remember this because when students are 'set' or 'streamed' within a particular year group, the differences in their ability may not be as pronounced as you might think. Part of this could be to do with the selection criteria by which students are set for ability.

Within many secondary schools, it is common for students to be set or streamed for at least some of their classes. Successive governments have argued for the educational benefits of such an approach but schools, it seems, have been a little more reluctant. Under a Freedom of Information request in 2010, the DfE reported that only 40% of lessons observed by Ofsted inspectors were either set or streamed (leaving the vast majority of lessons being taught in mixed-ability classes). So, like the organisation of students in year groups which has been done for organisational reasons rather than educational ones, the arguments for the benefits of setting or streaming seem to be highly contestable. These have tended to fall into two main areas of consideration: the academic and social. In terms of the social arguments, Richard Hatcher has observed that:

> The most overt mechanisms of social differentiation within the school system arise from processes of selection, both between schools, as a result of parental choice and school admissions procedures, *and within schools, as a result of forms of grouping students*. (Hatcher 1998, p. 494) [my italics]

Schools also seem to understand the academic arguments which indicate that minority and disadvantaged students tend to be over-represented in lower-level classes (Gamoran 2002) and that the pressure placed on students in higher sets or streams can often be overwhelming (Boaler et al. 2000). However, the arguments in favour of such approaches should not be dismissed too readily. During interviews, teachers told Smith and Sutherland that setting or streaming students helped them because:

- They were dealing with a smaller range of ability.

- They could sort out students with behavioural problems so that at least some could have a chance to learn.

- More able students could be challenged more easily.

▨ Mixed-ability teaching encouraged, in their view, teaching to the middle and was therefore inappropriate for a good number of students in the class. (Smith and Sutherland 2003, p. 142)

However students are grouped within the school, please remember my maxim that if you are teaching more than one student at a time, then your teaching is, in a fundamental way, aimed at a mixed-ability class. As I will consider below, personalisation, and the closely related pedagogical strategy of differentiation, are key elements of every lesson plan. The individual needs of specific students, or groups of students, will not be met by accident. As we discussed in the previous chapter that focused on assessment, you will need to make deliberate choices about your specific differentiation techniques to ensure that every student within your class has the opportunity to learn in the most effective way.

PRACTICAL TASK

Consider the ways that students are grouped within your school or teaching placement. Make a list of the most common approaches. Why are certain areas of the curriculum dealt with in a different way to others? Is this for pragmatic or educational reasons? More generally, have you observed any differences in the educational performance of older or younger students within a particular academic year? How can you mitigate the influence of a student's age on their academic performance?

Lesson planning stage eight: differentiating appropriately

Differentiation is the pedagogical term that teachers use to describe how they seek to make things different for each student's specific learning needs in their classroom. As we will see below, differentiation is closely allied to personalisation. Some teachers and educational theorists use the two terms interchangeably. But I think that the two terms do mean something slightly different, hence my dealing with them separately here. For me, differentiation is about your pedagogy. Personalisation, as we will see, relates to a strategy that may extend beyond your classroom and involve others across the school (and also the wider community).

Defining differentiation

At the heart of the term 'differentiation' are two notions both related to the root of the word; first, students are all *different*; second, teachers need to make *different* pedagogical choices depending on what they think is the best way that their students can learn. Differentiation is best conceived of as a specific set of pedagogical strategies. It is not a random process and nor can it be left to chance in your classroom. As Tomlinson describes, it can be conceived of as a process of engagement with your students and their learning that is cyclical in design:

Effective differentiation is based on a clear cycle of:

- Articulating what is essential in a topic or discipline.

- Assessing a student's standing relative to those essentials.

- Providing feedback and adapting instruction to ensure that each student progresses in the most effective ways possible to master the essentials.

- Assessing outcomes.

- Making additional adaptations as needed. (Tomlinson 2005, p. 264)

Before we examine some of the specific differentiation strategies that you may want to develop in your teaching, we will pause for a moment and consider each of these steps in a little more detail.

What is essential?

Before you can differentiate sensibly, you need to know what it is that you want to differentiate. This will involve you reflecting on the subject matter that you are teaching in a structured way. As we have seen through Chapter 2 (when we considered the planning of learning objectives and learning outcomes) and Chapter 3 (when we looked at the design of teaching activities), the development of your understanding about the subject you are teaching and how the various elements of potential learning contained within it need to be sequenced in a meaningful way.

When teachers talk about the subject content of a lesson, and the learning they are hoping will be achieved, they often use terms like the *depth* and *breadth* of the curriculum. Clearly, at certain points in any one given lesson, you may be trying to cover quite a lot of curriculum content (more of a focus on 'breadth') whilst at other moments in a lesson you may want to be digging down into quite a lot of detail about a particular issue (more of a focus on 'depth').

This question about what is essential in a topic or discipline is, therefore, heavily contextualised by your lesson plan and the sequencing of subject content within it, as well as the speed by which you want to teach key concepts or processes that you have identified. Remember that your learning objectives, and their associated outcomes, will be reflecting what students are going to be learning through completing the activities you have constructed (just 'doing' them does not necessarily mean that they are going to learn anything); therefore, the word 'essential' here relates to an aspect of learning not to the activity itself. The key question is what is the essential learning contained within the lesson that I want to differentiate so that all students can engage with it?

Where are your students starting from?

Tomlinson's second point is that your strategies for differentiation need to take account of where students are starting from. This might be within the context of a sequence of learning that they have undertaken in a previous lesson. Or, it might be at a broader level of their work throughout one unit of work and how that might link to the sequence of lessons that you are currently planning; we will consider this scenario further in Chapter 7. Either way (and it will probably be both), it is important that you have an understanding of their learning 'journey' and can place specific strategies for differentiation and support at meaningful places along their future path. As we mentioned in Chapter 3, if you do not know where you are going, any road will take you there. If you are not able to predict, even in a general way, the path of a student's learning, then it is unlikely that you are going to be able to use a differentiation strategy to help support their learning in anything other than the most general of ways. The ability to differentiate learning successfully relies on the knowledge you have of individual students. It is much better to plan for differentiation with specific students in mind rather than try to do it abstractly.

Providing feedback and adapting instruction

The contextualisation of a student's learning within a subject, and within their specific learning journey, will lead to action on your part. As we explore the specifics of different approaches to differentiation below, this will involve you providing feedback, adapting instructions and a lot more besides in order to ensure that each student progresses in the most effective way and engages with the learning objectives that you have set.

Assessing outcomes and making adaptations

As we considered in the previous chapter, using a range of assessment strategies (with a particular focus on assessment for learning techniques) is the most effective way of assessing students' work and judging the effectiveness of your teaching. We will be considering these issues further in Chapter 9 when we turn our attention to how you evaluate and reflect on your teaching.

REFLECTIVE TASK

Before you read on, spend a few moments thinking about the various forms of differentiation that you have observed in the work of other teachers. Can you identify any of the key points made above in respect of their work? More practically, what did they actually do to help differentiate the learning objectives they had set so that all students could engage with them throughout their lesson? We will be exploring this further below.

Types of differentiation

Within this broad set of ideas that have placed the strategies of differentiation within a cyclical process, it is now possible to highlight and discuss a number of specific strategies and techniques by which you can differentiate your students' learning. These ideas have all come from my reading, my own teaching and my observation of other teachers over the years. Within some subject areas, certain approaches may be more common than others. But I have seen all these techniques or strategies used in both primary and secondary school classrooms. They are not presented in any order of importance, although I would say that the first two 'types' are more common in my experience than the others. Please also remember that it is seldom going to be the case that any one approach or strategy is going to be used in isolation from the others. There will be a considerable degree of overlap in some cases.

Differentiation by task

Differentiation by task involves you choosing different tasks for different students or different groups of students, all within your overall lesson plan. This can be a major commitment and would involve you having to undertake a considerable amount of planning. As Burton observes:

> Differentiation by task requires a great deal of forward planning by teachers and a thorough knowledge of each learner's needs. Whilst commercially produced material can be of some value, case-study research has shown that teachers still need to devise their own differentiated support materials to meet each student's needs. (Burton 2003, p. 59)

In one lesson that I observed recently, the Mathematics teacher differentiated by task in order to target specific support at a group of students who were struggling to grasp the key principles behind multiplying and dividing fractions. In order to do this, he divided the class into four key groups based on the students' abilities in this area. Three of the groups were given tailored activities together with various forms of support; the fourth group was taught directly by him for a period of the lesson before the whole class came back together for a plenary activity. This was a successful lesson in that it allowed certain students to work independently (but still with support), whilst other students received intensive support from the teacher in a way that would have been difficult if other forms of differentiation were being used.

Differentiation by task requires you to have planned carefully what the overall learning aims and objectives will entail, and then have worked out different pathways through this for groups of students within your class. At any one given moment, specific groups of students may be working on very different tasks from other students within the class. This has significant consequences for the provision of resources and will also impact on other areas of your work (e.g. it might not be possible to assess the students' work in the same way, thereby requiring thought to be given towards an alternative assessment strategy). As Burton notes, the design of the teaching activities for each group is only part of the differentiated provision. You will also need to think carefully about the support materials and frameworks within each task to ensure that students can progress appropriately. For all these reasons, I would suggest that differentiation by task, although one of the most obvious ways to differentiate, should be used sparingly.

Differentiation by outcome

In a simple way, differentiation by outcome is really the opposite of differentiation by task. Differentiation by outcome is when all students undertake the same task but, as one might guess, produce different pieces of work from this. Whilst this is a much more manageable form of differentiation and may not require you to do as much planning as if you were adopting the differentiation by task approach, it still needs to be very carefully handled. This is because there is a natural and perhaps inevitable tendency for classroom work to produce differentiation by outcome anyway, without you planning for very much at all! Clearly, this is unsatisfactory and will not stand up to scrutiny.

Within my main subject area, Music, differentiation by outcome is a common strategy. Here, it is used because it allows and facilitates a range of creative responses that is entirely suitable for the subject itself. In one recent lesson I taught, students were learning how to play a samba beat. I taught the class a four-part samba beat using key rhythms and then asked them to work in small groups, coordinating the rhythms and using variations in dynamics (volume), texture (the combination of instruments playing together) and structure to create an interesting beat to play to the class. Within the class of around 30 students, numerous different versions of the samba beat resulted, some played more convincingly than others! However, the creative choices that students made could only have been facilitated by giving those students some creative ownership of the task itself.

If you are choosing to use differentiation by outcome as a strategy, then you need to spend a considerable amount of time thinking about how you will support the identified learning outcomes on your lesson plan. At their most basic (as we saw in Chapter 2), this might include you designating outcomes using the 'all, most and few' categories. If this is the case, you will need to think about how your strategy for differentiation by outcome supports students in at least these three main outcome areas. You need to show how you will make a difference to their learning, seeking to promote it to the highest level whenever possible. Specifically, this might involve you:

- Setting more open extension activities within the core task for some groups of stronger students because you know that these may be interpreted and explored in a more demanding way by these students.

▨ Using a different range of resources, support and questioning strategies with certain groups of students for specific reasons (of which more below).

▨ Varying either the time allocated to the task or the process by which specific groups of students work within a common task for specific reasons.

▨ Providing a range of frameworks for the task depending on the student or group of students, again, with a specific reason in mind.

Differentiation by resource

Differentiation by resource can mean a number of different things. First, it could be that you differentiate using different physical resources such as worksheets, software packages, or other forms of instructional materials. These would be used at the same time in the class with different students or groups of students. In a way this could be seen as a variation on differentiation by task, but with the notable difference that the students can be doing the same thing but learning through the use of different materials. Spend a few minutes flicking back through Chapter 4 and look at the range of resources that you have at your disposal in the classroom. Each of these can be used as a potential opportunity or tool for differentiation. For example, why not consider how a simple wall display could become a differentiated resource for students? Done well, differentiation by resource can free up considerable periods of time for you within your lesson that you can then devote to other things.

Differentiation by support

As we discussed in Chapter 4, the use of other adults in the classroom can be very beneficial. Within this context, it will be vital that your lesson plan shows how you can use other adults in a differentiated way, making decisions about how they will spend their time with a specific student or group of students and for what purpose. Clearly, this is best done through some form of collaboration but there may be times when you just have to make a decision about this and let your colleague know at the beginning of the lesson what they will be doing and why.

There may also be occasions when you want to make use of the students as a resource to help differentiate the learning opportunities. This might include buddying up students in groups for specific reasons. Working off the well-known principle that the best way to learn how to do something yourself is to teach it to others, there may be justifiable occasions when you want to ask specific students to help support other students within the class for a particular purpose. I would encourage you not to do this too often with the same students though.

In the example I gave above from a Mathematics lesson, in addition to differentiating by task, the teacher was also differentiating the forms of support that certain students received for a portion of the lesson. His own, direct input was one form of support; other forms of support included pre-prepared worksheets and other online resources.

Interestingly, in recent years I have seen a few examples of the year group structure of schools being dismantled as older students (perhaps in their final year of schooling) work with younger students as part of their advanced level studies. This can work very effectively but, as with all strategies for differentiation, needs careful planning by the teacher.

Differentiation by questioning

Questioning is a vital skill. It is beyond the scope of this book to go into too much detail on this particular aspect of your pedagogy, but it is hard to over-emphasise the importance of being able to ask skilful questions of your students as a strategy for both differentiating their learning and assessing their achievements in a particular lesson. Questions can be differentiated through the use of various frameworks. One of the most commonly seen in education is Bloom's taxonomy. Although it was not designed for this purpose, it has been taken and adapted by many writers to help give teachers a range of question stems that they can use to develop students' understanding to the next 'level'. So, for instance, basic remembering questions such as 'What happened after . . .?' or 'Which is true or false . . .?' could be developed into questions that help students evaluate things, such as 'What choice would you have made about . . .?' or 'Who will gain and who will lose if . . .?'

Differentiation by learning style

Differentiation by learning style has, perhaps, some of the closest links to personalisation (which I will discuss below). For now, it is suffice to say that commonly designated learning styles, such as visual, auditory and kinaesthetic learning, could be used to usefully differentiate a particular concept or topic that you are wanting to address in a lesson. However, I need to issue a big educational health warning here! Do not build a differentiation or personalisation strategy based on the pseudo-psychology behind this way of educational thinking. I do not believe that students can be categorised as being visual, auditory or kinaesthetic learners; nor is it helpful to do so. However, it may be helpful from the perspective of your work to think about how your pedagogy could adopt a more visual, more auditory or more kinaesthetic approach, or indeed how you might vary this for specific students or groups of students, as one aspect of an approach towards differentiation.

These six strategies present a broad range of approaches through which you can vary your pedagogy to support students' learning in a deliberate and structured way. Whether it be through task formation, through the provision of different resources, the skilful use of questioning, by varying the time you spend with specific individuals, or by utilising the support of other adults in specific way, differentiated approaches can help develop, sustain and extend your students' learning very powerfully.

A word of warning

At this point, I would like to issue one word of caution. Differentiation of this type is not about producing different lesson plans for each individual in the class. Tomlinson points this out, when she comments that:

> while it is true that differentiated instruction offers several avenues to learning, it does not assume a separate level for each learner . . . Effective differentiated classrooms include purposeful student movement and some purposeful student talking. (Tomlinson 2001 p. 2)

Although differentiation does include the grouping and movement of students, alongside purposeful strategies to get them talking in different ways about their work, it does not mean an overbearing requirement for you to personalise everything in micro detail. Nor, I might add, is it a recipe for classroom disorder, with individuals undertaking unrelated tasks or activities. Differentiation is an approach to teaching and learning which uses materials, resources, plans, or tasks in a strategic way to help you to help your students achieve their individual potential in your lesson.

PRACTICAL TASK

Which of the differentiation strategies described above do you feel most comfortable with at this point? Think about a lesson that you are going to be teaching in the near future and write a couple of sentences that describe your approach to differentiation for that lesson. Make sure that you focus it around specific students in your class. Add this short paragraph to your lesson plan.

For future lessons, experiment with alternative approaches to differentiation. When trying something new, make sure that you think hard after the lesson about the successes or limitations of the new approach. Write about it in your lesson evaluation.

Personalisation

Strategies of differentiation will be your primary focus in lesson planning. Differentiation, for me, is about your actions as a teacher. It is about your choice of a pedagogical strategy, or strategies, for use within a lesson. It is something that is rightly under your control. This is why I have discussed it first. However, in recent years the term 'personalisation' has entered the educational discourse and I need to address this here. For some, personalisation has displaced differentiation. However, my view is that they are distinct yet related concepts. It is interesting to see how others have interpreted these two terms.

For Bray (2013), differentiation is contrasted with personalisation by who is involved in doing it. Differentiation is under the control of the teacher; personalisation is driven by the learner. Table 6.1 presents some interesting comparisons for us to consider.

Whilst I find myself agreeing with many of her assertions about personalisation, I find myself disagreeing with her reflections on differentiation which seem, to me, to be based on a very limited view of what a teacher could and should do. As with any set of binaries, the truth is probably found somewhere in between or even within both statements. But what Bray's attributes do emphasise, and which I agree with, is that personalisation is about a broader system of educational opportunity

Table 6.1 Bray's categorisation of personalisation and differentiation

Personalisation	Differentiation
The learner . . .	*The teacher . . .*
Drives their learning.	Provides instruction to groups of learners.
Connects learning with interests, talents, passions and aspirations.	Adjusts learning needs for groups of learners.
Owns and is responsible for their learning that includes their voice and choice on how and what they learn.	Is responsible for a variety of instruction for different groups of learners.
Identifies goals for their learning and benchmarks as they progress along their learning path with guidance from the teacher.	Identifies the same objectives for different groups of learners.
Develops the skills to select and use the appropriate technology and resources to support and enhance their learning.	Selects technology and resources to support the learning needs of different groups of learners.
Builds a network of peers, experts, and teachers to guide and support their learning.	Supports groups of learners who are reliant on them to support their learning.
Becomes a self-directed, expert learner who monitors progress and reflects on learning based on mastery of content and skills.	Uses data and assessments to modify teaching and provides feedback for groups and individual learners to advance their learning.

that students can thrive within and, eventually, take ownership of their own learning through. Whilst differentiation is a strategy that begins and remains with the teacher and their planning, personalisation is something that might begin with the teacher or school and then quickly move into the domain of the student.

Gilbert defines personalisation as:

> Taking a highly structured and responsive approach to each child's and young person's learning, in order that all are able to progress, achieve and participate. It means strengthening the link between learning and teaching by engaging students – and their parents – as partners in learning. (DCSF 2007, p. 6)

As any teacher will tell you (and I am sure you have realised by now), every student has their own specific educational needs. As we have discussed already, differentiation is not about producing an individual lesson or learning plan for every student. What does Gilbert mean by saying that personalisation is about 'engaging students as partners in learning'? For me, it is about roles and responsibilities. Personalisation places some, if not eventually all, of the responsibility back onto the student to begin to make sense of the educational opportunities that are available to them through your teaching. It empowers them in their role as a learner, rather than them being seen as passive recipients of 'stuff' that you might present them with. For schools, it is about creating a broader culture of learning that engages with students in a much more proactive way, seeking to pass some of the responsibility for their learning onto them, rather than seeing it solely as a demand on its teachers; it is also about them being explicit in the demands it makes on individuals to take responsibility for their own actions within that learning culture.

This way of thinking about education has exhibited itself in many forms in recent years. Within music education, for example, the 'Musical Futures' movement has sought to relocate decisions about the content of the music curriculum away from the teacher and back to the students' control. In a typical Musical Futures lesson, students will choose their own song to learn to sing or play, rather than being led through something that the teacher has chosen. Rather than being seen as a denigration of the teacher's role, advocates for this type of approach would argue that the teacher's role is a more skilful one of facilitation and nurturing, spotting and supporting the development of skills and understanding as they emerge within a context of personalised learning, rather than seeking to force knowledge, skills and other musical content onto unwilling minds.

One of the most important elements of personalisation that you will want to explore early in your teaching career will be related to your curriculum planning. This is twofold. First, it is about planning for personalised content in your lessons. This will allow students a greater degree of say in respect of the 'what' of the curriculum at certain points in a unit of work. Second, it is about the 'how' in respect of how they are going to learn in your lessons. This is a very important distinction to get hold of. One teacher described it to me as being like a 'doorway into learning'. Whilst you will inevitably only have a partial understanding of where your students are all at, individually, given the right opportunities and motivation they will be able to take up opportunities for learning and personalise these in ways that you could never foresee. To this end, personalisation involves planning for a range of learning opportunities, considering their ability levels, looking at the structure of tasks (e.g. open or closed), the types of presentational approaches you might adopt (e.g. explanations or modelling), the progression routes within the learning that you might expect, the particular resources you want to use (or might expect students to use), and much more besides. In one word, it is 'flexibility'.

Strategies for differentiation and personalisation will both need to be considered within your lesson plan. I would suggest that you start by considering differentiation. Strategies for personalisation will flow naturally from this as you become more confident in the planning process.

But in addition to these two vital areas, there will be students in your classes who will require you to make specific and very detailed interventions in order for their education to advance. I am referring specifically to students with special educational needs.

Lesson planning stage nine: addressing students with SEN

'Special Educational Needs' (SEN) is a term used to describe the needs of a student who has a difficulty or disability that makes learning harder for them than it might be for other students of their age. It is a legal term that covers a broad spectrum of difficulties and disabilities. Many students will have a special educational need at some point in their education. As a teacher, it is your responsibility to work as part of a team to support these students, adopting and implementing specific strategies to help them engage with the curriculum you have developed.

There are numerous 'types' or 'categories' of special educational needs. It is beyond the scope of this book to discuss them all, but some of the most common types or categories of SEN that you may come across in your school include:

- Attention deficit hyperactivity disorder (ADHD)

- Asperger's syndrome

- Autism

- Dyslexia

▧ Emotional and behavioural difficulties (EBD)

▧ Epilepsy

▧ Obsessive compulsive disorder (OCD)

▧ Speech and language disorder

▧ Tourette's syndrome.

You can find a very helpful and comprehensive list and description of many different SEN at www.specialeducationalneeds.co.uk/typesofsen-disability.htm.

The provisions that you will need to make to support a student with SEN will be detailed within a whole school policy. This policy will contain a range of statements of which you must be aware. Indicative statements might include phrases such as:

▧ The right of the child to have their SEN met through a broad, well-balanced and relevant education.

▧ The right of the child and their parents to have their views listened to, taken into account and acted on if they are in their best interests.

▧ The incorporation of children with SEN into mainstream schooling whenever and wherever possible, sometimes with the assistance of outside specialists working collaboratively with the school.

Normally, a student with SEN will have gone through a formal process whereby their SEN will have been identified through the production of a formal statement. These vary from school to school, and local area to local area. Once a child with SEN has been formally identified through the relevant process, schools will normally write an Individual Education Plan to help formulate a coherent approach to that child's educational entitlement in the school. This IEP would normally include:

▧ What special or additional help is going to be given to that particular child.

▧ Who will provide that help and how often will it be delivered.

▧ What help can the parents give their child at home to support the work being done by you and other teachers within the school.

▧ The setting of some individual targets for that child's progress during the term or academic year.

▧ A description of how and when the child's progress will be checked or assessed.

In respect of your work as an individual classroom teacher, all this preparatory work in forming a student's IEP will have gone on previously and will probably not have involved you at all. However, once put in place, it is your responsibility to respond to this plan and show how the planning that you are doing, lesson by lesson, will help that student meet the demands of their IEP. Part of this planning process will include you helping to identify and diagnose particular issues within your subject area(s) as soon as possible; it will also include you having to adopt or adapt alternative teaching strategies in light of the individual needs that a particular student might have in your class. This may involve you using different differentiation strategies for specific students. To give some practical examples, students with SEN may need additional help with:

- General work within your classes including reading, writing, number work or understanding information. This might require you to amend or adapt the resources that you are using to assist them in a specific way.

- Expressing themselves or understanding what others are saying. This may result in you having to consider the social groupings in your class and the ways in which students engage with each other in different activities.

- Making friends or relating to adults. Perhaps this is an aspect of support that extends beyond your individual classroom and will affect how these students are integrated into the life of the whole school.

Teaching gifted and talented pupils

The definition of students as being either 'gifted' or 'talented' has rather fallen off the educational policy agenda in recent years. Through the late 1990s and early 2000s all schools were required to produce a register of gifted and talented students and make specific provision for their educational requirements. Various other initiatives such as the establishment of the National Academy for Gifted and Talented Youth at the University of Warwick were established and supported the work of schools in this area. Sadly, the coalition government abolished this soon after coming to power in 2010.

For many teachers, being talented or gifted in a particular area of academic study was something that required this degree of specialist and specialised support. Whilst the notion of a 'list' of students with particular gifts or talents has fallen by the wayside in most schools today, there will be students in the classes that you teach who show an exceptional ability for your subject. You will need to consider what individual provision needs to be made for these students and plan for this accordingly in your lesson plan.

Van Tassell-Baska's work (1998) provides a useful framework as you begin to consider your work in this area. Her curriculum theory for gifted and talented pupils identifies four key attributes that you can begin to consider:

1 The level of the curriculum.

2 The pace of the curriculum.

3 The complexity of the curriculum.

4 The depth of the curriculum.

The level of the curriculum refers to the way that the curriculum content that you choose should interest and challenge gifted or talented students. In some ways, it relates to the most basic differentiation strategies discussed above including differentiation by task and outcome. Her argument here is that the level of curriculum content, and how it is presented through your lesson's teaching episodes and activities, must be at a suitable level for high-achieving students.

The pace of the curriculum refers to your delivery style in the classroom. As we have seen in various ways throughout this book, your teaching pace can vary, almost minute by minute, in the classroom and can certainly be used to help maintain the flow of learning within a lesson. But it is also an integral part of effective differentiation. Van Tassell-Baska argues that your gifted and talented students will be able to maintain a higher pace of learning than your average students. Given that you are unlikely to be teaching your gifted or talented students as a separate group, the key here is to find ways to facilitate a faster pace of learning for some, whilst acknowledging that others may require more time on a specific topic. In order to do this well, you will need to employ more sophisticated types of differentiation.

Van Tassell-Baska's third point refers to the complexity of the curriculum. Here, she asks us to focus on the capacity of gifted and talented students to engage in a number of advanced-level ideas simultaneously. Challenging gifted and talented students at the level of ideas and advanced cognitive thinking is not new. However, it is important that you differentiate this from standard curriculum content and this will require a separate degree of lesson planning for these pupils.

Finally, Van Tassell-Baska's concept of the depth of the curriculum relates to the opportunity of allowing gifted and talented students to spend time exploring an area of interest to higher levels, perhaps even reaching the level of an expert in a particular field of enquiry. Many gifted and talented pupils will show a considerable degree of intrinsic motivation and engagement when a topic or theme grabs their attention. They will want to run with this, explore it and mine it for new information. Allowing time for this when it occurs is difficult to plan for, but as with any element of lesson planning you should be alert to this and flexible in your pedagogy when it happens. Within many lessons, there may not be the time available for this type of in-depth study. But it is important to recognise when an individual student has made that particular type of connection with a topic or set of ideas. Outside the lesson itself, there will be opportunities to develop their thinking further, perhaps through an extended homework task or another kind of extra-curricular experience. I would also suggest that you try to revisit the specific area of interest, or at least provide signposts to it, in future lessons so that the student's interest is supported and developed in a systematic way.

Summary

Effective teaching and learning is centred on a strong relationship between the individual teacher, their emerging pedagogy and their students. All students desire an education that is appropriately personalised to their educational needs. Every child matters and their education is too important to be squashed into a one-size-fits-all box. Early in your teaching career, commit to focusing on your role in the classroom, honing and crafting your pedagogy and listening carefully to your students. Prioritise the development of a range of approaches to differentiation in your work. These are the keys to an effective, personal approach to teaching and learning.

Further reading

Wilmot, E. (2006) *Personalising Learning in the Primary Classroom: A Practical Guide for Teachers and School Leaders.* Carmarthen: Crown House Publishing.

Do not be put off by the word primary in the above book title. There is much of value in this book for all teachers, regardless of the age of the students they are teaching.

References

Boaler, J., Wiliam, D. and Brown, M. (2000) 'Students' experiences of ability grouping: Disaffection, polarisation and the construction of failure'. *British Educational Research Journal*, 26:5, 631–48.

Bray, B. (2013) Personalisation vs differentiation vs individualisation. http://barbarabray.net/2012/01/22/personalization-vs-differentiation-vs-individualization-chart/ (accessed 5 October 2013).

Burton, D. (2003) 'Differentiation of schooling and pedagogy'. In Bartlett, S. and Burton, D. (eds) *Education Studies: Essential Issues.* London: Sage, pp. 42–71.

Crawford, C., Dearden, L. and Greaves, E. (2011) Does when you are born matter? The impact of month of birth on children's cognitive and non-cognitive skills in England. www.ifs.org.uk/bns/bn122.pdf (accessed 4 July 2012).

DCSF (2007) *Pedagogy and Personalisation.* London: DCSF. Also online: www.standards.dcsf.gov.uk/primary/publications/learning_and_teaching/pedagogy_personalisation (accessed 12 May 2010).

DfE (Department for Education) (2012) Streamlining within English comprehensive schools. http://education.gov.uk/aboutdfe/foi/disclosuresaboutschools/a0068565/streamlining-within-english-comprehensive-schools (accessed 18 September 2012).

Field, S., Kuczera, M. and Pont, B. (2007) *No More Failures: Ten Steps to Equity in Education.* Paris: OECD. Also online: www.oecd.org/dataoecd/49/16/49623744.pdf (accessed 5 July 2012).

Gamoran, A. (2002) *Standards, Inequality & Ability Grouping in Schools.* Centre for Educational Sociology, University of Edinburgh.

Hatcher, R. (1998) 'Labour, official school improvement and equality'. *Journal of Education Policy*, 13:4, 485–99.

Ireson, J. and Hallam, S. (2001) *Ability Grouping in Education*. London: Paul Chapman.

Palmer, P. (2009) www.newhorizons.org/strategies/character/palmer.htm (accessed 2 October 2013).

Skyes, E., Bell, J. and Rodeiro, C. (2009) 'Birthdate effects: A review of the literature from 1990-on'. www.cambridgeassessment.org.uk/ca/digitalAssets/169664_Cambridge_Lit_ Review_Birthdate_d3.pdf (accessed 5 July 2012).

Smith, C. M. M. and Sutherland, M. J. (2003) 'Setting or mixed ability? Teachers' views of the organisation of students for learning'. *Journal of Research in Special Educational Needs*, 3:3, 141–6.

Tomlinson, C. A. (2005) 'Grading and differentiation: Paradox or good practice?' *Theory Into Practice*, 44:3, 262–9.

Tomlinson, C. A. (2001) *How to Differentiate Instruction in Mixed-ability Classrooms*. Alexandria, VA: Association for Supervision & Curriculum Development.

Van Tassell-Baska, J. (1998) *Excellence in Educating Gifted and Talented Learners* (3rd edition). Denver: Love Publishing.

7 Documenting your planning

Introduction

Up to this point in the book, no specific planning documentation has been introduced. Perhaps you think that this is a curious omission? After all, planning needs to be contextualised within a lesson planning document doesn't it? I agree entirely. However, my rationale here has been to look at each of the key issues involved in lesson planning rather than getting hung up too early on what needs to be written down within a particular document. The nine key issues or stages that we have examined so far are:

- Lesson planning stage one: Defining your learning objective(s) (Chapter 2)

- Lesson planning stage two: Defining your learning outcomes (Chapter 2)

- Lesson planning stage three: The three-part lesson (Chapter 3)

- Lesson planning stage four: The classroom environment (Chapter 4)

- Lesson planning stage five: Your classroom resources (Chapter 4)

- Lesson planning stage six: Your assessment strategy (Chapter 5)

- Lesson planning stage seven: Construct a positive classroom environment (Chapter 5)

- Lesson planning stage eight: Differentiating appropriately (Chapter 6)

- Lesson planning stage nine: Addressing students with SEN (Chapter 6).

At the outset of this chapter, I would like to state, clearly and unambiguously, that there is no one, single version of a lesson plan document that you must use in your teaching. For this reason, I will not be advocating the use of any one version of a lesson plan document in this book. Rather, I will be outlining a version of a lesson plan document that you might consider using and adapting as befits your own teaching and the school within which you are working. Please take advice from other professionals who know you, your school and, in the case of student teachers, your training provider too, in making choices about the particular lesson planning form that you are going to adopt.

The purpose of this chapter is to apply the nine key stages (and associated principles) outlined in the early chapters to help you make an informed choice about the documentation for your planning in light of the context within which you are working. I will also discuss here how the individual lesson plan itself relates to broader processes of medium- and longer-term curriculum planning (such as 'unit of work' documentation) and the differences in planning approaches that you can expect to find in primary and secondary schools. For various reasons, that will become apparent as the chapter progresses, I am going to start with what are known as the long- and medium-term planning documents.

The long- and medium-term plan

Long- and medium-term planning is vitally important. I am starting with this because it is crucial to understand how the teaching and learning that takes place in an individual lesson is part of a sequence of lessons that students will engage with over time. In a typical secondary school, this might be through their weekly lessons in a particular subject; in a primary school, this might be through a particular topic that has been chosen and developed for a term's work. As we will consider below, the differences between these two contexts play an important influence in shaping how this planning process occurs, but there is enough in common between them to talk about a general process of long- and medium-term planning here.

I would like to suggest a two-staged process for you to consider as you start your work in this area. The first stage involves the construction of a 'curriculum overview map'; the second stage will introduce a 'unit of work map'. Both stages are drawn from the work of teachers who I have interviewed about their planning processes in primary and secondary schools over the last year.

Stage one: developing a curriculum overview map

A curriculum overview map provides you with an opportunity to sketch out a long-term plan for a particular key stage. Figure 7.1 shows an example drawn from the work of one primary school at Key Stage 2.

On one side of A4 paper, Figure 7.1 provides a snapshot of learning for a year group within the Key Stage 2 curriculum. It contains the following basic elements:

- A term-by-term representation of the various topics or themes contained within the year.
- An opportunity to describe the purpose of the chosen topics or themes in light of the chosen themes.
- An identification of the key learning challenges that the topics/themes contain.
- An indication of the specific pedagogies that might be included at key moments throughout the year.

Year 4	Term 1		Term 2		Term 3	
Key Topics						
Purpose						
Key Learning Challenges						
Specific Pedagogies						

Literacy Units	Numeracy Units	Science	ICT	RE
PE	Music	Art	PSHE	Design Technology

Figure 7.1 Curriculum overview map (primary)

■ A subject-by-subject breakdown where the specific contributions of each subject area can be identified. These will often contain references to the National Curriculum programmes of study for the relevant subject area.

Figure 7.2 shows an exemplar long-term planning form from the work of a secondary school music teacher. As you look at this, ask yourself what similarities there are with Figure 7.1.

In Figure 7.2, the long-term curriculum overview map allows you to represent the key topics in your subject throughout a key stage. It contains:

■ The title of each unit of work for each term.

■ The key purposes for each unit of work.

■ The key learning that each unit of work will contain (these will become the important link to the individual learning objectives for each lesson).

■ An identification of the key pedagogical approaches that might be used within each unit of work.

■ A reminder about the key concepts that are underpinning the subject in question (in this case Music). Please note that 'key concepts' were an important part of the previous National Curriclum but in the most recent revision in 2013 these have sadly been dropped from the official Programmes of Study.

One of the key similarities between Figure 7.1 and Figure 7.2 is that you need to write concisely. Although electronic documents can be expanded infinitely, in the best planning that I saw from teachers using these curriculum overview maps the completed maps were seldom more than two pages in total. Conciseness is the key. If you adopt these forms, keep your responses within each of the boxes very focused. The curriculum overview map is not the time or place for extended expositions of, or justifications for, your chosen topics and other responses. Keep it brief!

But whilst conciseness is key in terms of the actual writing of the curriculum overview map, the amount of work that goes into this document is considerable. It will require you to give it a lot of time and careful thought. One of the key questions that you will want to consider in relation to your curriculum overview map is 'How does it allow for and facilitate students' cognitive development over time?' In order to answer this question, you will need to have a clear understanding of the common pathways of cognitive development within your subject area. These are pathways that you should have been introduced to as part of your formal training to become a teacher. Developmental psychology is a massive field that is beyond the boundary of this book to consider in much depth. But, as we considered in some detail in Chapter 2, it is important for you to have obtained a broad understanding of how key knowledge, skills and understanding in your specialist subject area(s) develop. The curriculum overview map is the document on which your understanding of these processes is brought to life in the selection of key units of work that your students will study in order to develop these key attributes over the course of a whole key stage.

Year	Unit of Work	Term 1	Term 2	Term 3	Term 4	Term 5	Term 6
7	Unit Title						
	Purpose						
	Key Learning						
	Key Pedagogy						
8	Unit Title						
	Purpose						
	Key Learning						
	Key Pedagogy						
9	Unit Title						
	Purpose						
	Key Learning						
	Key Pedagogy						

Key Concepts:

Integrating Musical Processes	Cultural Awareness	Critical Thinking	Being Creative	Communicating

Figure 7.2 Curriculum overview map (secondary)

One of the simplest ways to consider this is to apply the twin but related concepts of 'depth' and 'breadth' to your curriculum overview map. You may remember that we used these concepts in our discussion of differentiation in Chapter 6. So when you are considering the completion of a curriculum overview map in a chosen subject area or for a particular year group, as well as the sequence of topics that you will include in each year, also consider the breadth and depth of learning that each unit might entail. Both can be treated flexibly – for example, you may want to give breadth to certain units of work, perhaps to ensure a blend of content across a year, but you will also want to study some key content within specific units in greater depth – and perhaps even revisit this key content within different units of work. I would suggest that you consider the following key points:

- Think about the curriculum as a spiral within which certain key concepts, skills, and knowledge may be introduced in one unit, at an early point in the year, and then be revisited and built upon later (in another unit later in the year).

- Simple content can be taught to students of all ages in different ways. I am sure that you can think of several topic areas which can be usefully taught to younger children but which can also be studied in greater depth in higher education settings. Try not to limit your choice of content to what you or others might perceive to be 'suitable' for a particular age group. There are many benefits to thinking laterally here and not conforming to traditional approaches.

- Break down subject knowledge in different ways. Try to prioritise the key knowledge, skills and understanding that are essential features of a topic area at an early stage. Please do not feel that you need to do everything in one go. Thinking about the curriculum as a whole allows you to make connections in all kinds of ways across the units of work that you are planning.

- Sequencing concepts, skills or knowledge is extremely important to ensure that students are not asked to do something cognitively complex without the basic cognitive skills being firmly established in their prior work. You will need to ensure that your planning, even at this level, is appropriately differentiated to ensure that all students can engage suitably in a particular unit of work.

- Learning itself is seldom uni-directional (otherwise we would tell a student something once and they'd remember it for ever!) and tends to follow complex patterns that are difficult to plan for systematically. The curriculum overview map, like any planning document, is just a plan and should not be stuck to religiously.

- Your classes are full of individual students who will have their own particular idiosyncrasies and will learn differently from the class you taught in a previous year. We would not expect your lesson planning, medium- or long-term planning to look the same each year (even though there may be similar elements contained within it). Keep the curriculum overview map under an annual review.

Having started with your subject, identified key areas of knowledge, concepts and skills, and worked towards completing your curriculum overview map, it is time to turn our focus to the next level of planning – the medium-term plan. For most teachers, regardless of whether they teach in a primary or secondary school, medium-term planning involves the writing of individual units of work.

Stage two: mapping the individual unit of work

The unit of work map relates directly to the curriculum overview map. Every unit on that map must be described within its own template document known as a unit of work. In most schools, primary or secondary, this will normally refer to a term's, or half a term's, work. However, in the primary school this could also refer to a particular topic (within which different subjects are combined) whilst within the secondary school this will probably refer to one discrete subject and the sequence of lessons within that subject.

I would strongly recommend that before you undertake the writing of a specific unit of work, you do a bit of brainstorming first. Within most schools that I visited in preparing for this book, this process was done collaboratively by a group of teachers. But it can be done individually too. Regardless of whether you are teaching in a primary or secondary school, the process of mapping out the unit of work using a simple chart can be very productive. The approach that I am going to share below came from the work of one music teacher in Cambridgeshire.

Figure 7.3 presents the start of the process of writing a unit of work using a typical brainstorming chart. As I describe the process as undertaken by this teacher, why not select one of the topics or themes that you might include within your own curriculum overview map and work through it using the following steps?

1 Place your topic title in the middle of the unit map. In my example, the teacher had chosen the topic of Gospel Music for his Year 7 class.

2 Surround the topic title with the top-level ideas drawn from your knowledge and understanding of your particular subject area. In the example I have provided, the teacher chose five key ideas drawn from an analysis he did of music, as a subject area, and the various key approaches that he considered the most important. These included elements such as 'cultural awareness', 'being creative', 'communicating'.

3 For each key idea that you have identified (and which you have placed around your topic title), identify and write some key questions that relate to the particular idea and how you might seek to explore it within that specific unit with your students. I have provided some example questions that this music teacher adopted. The questions that you write will help you explore the key concept ideas drawn from your own subject area within the context of your chosen unit of work. Please bear in mind that these questions came from the work of one music teacher and will probably not be applicable to your own work. But the key point is that you need to ask questions that interrogate your understanding of your subject area and result in provoking you, intellectually, to a practical and pedagogical response!

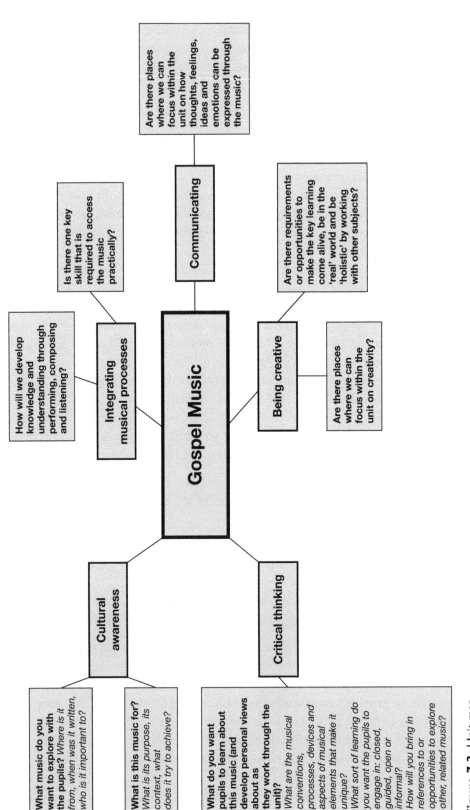

Figure 7.3 Unit map

4 Start the process of answering your questions in the final part of the brainstorming chart. Be succinct and concise. Your answers here will help you write
your own unit of work document. Within this final stage, you need to be very
practical and think about the key activities that will help your students engage
with the key ideas you have identified.

Writing the unit of work

The actual unit of work document flows from the kind of brainstorming activity
that I have described above. As I mentioned, in most cases the processes that
underpin medium-term planning are normally done by a group of teachers working
collaboratively. There are many benefits to this approach but, on occasions,
teachers do have to work on their own. If this is the case for you, I would strongly
recommend that you find another teacher who can act as 'critical friend' in this
planning process. In the early days of your teaching, this might be a university or
school mentor, or perhaps a trusted colleague working elsewhere in the school. The
critical support and feedback that these colleagues can give you will be invaluable.

As I have discussed throughout the book, individual lesson plans detail the
learning objectives, teaching activities, resources, assessment and differentiation
strategies for the individual lesson; the unit of work document provides an overview of the sequence of lessons that constitute a particular topic within your
curriculum overview map. In some schools, units of work are referred to as
'schemes of work'. There are numerous exemplar documents for these documents
available online. The best ones are short and concise, perhaps containing a one-
page overview of the unit followed by another one page that provides a short
summary of the various lessons that the unit contains. Figure 7.4 illustrates one
example of this from a primary school teacher's work in south Cheshire.

Units of work should contain the following:

▪ A *title* that is brief, concise and describes the unit of work. You can take this from
your unit map and transfer it to your unit of work template. In my example, the
teacher has used the term 'Area of Learning' as a title.

▪ A *broad description* of the unit of work, the key content or themes, and where it
sits within the broader long-term plan for the key stage within which it is placed.
Refer back to your curriculum overview map at this point and provide a simple
explanation of how this unit of work fits within the overall plan for the key stage
(i.e. why is it where it is?). In my example, this content would be contained
within the various subject-related areas (such as 'Communication, Language &
Literacy', 'Mathematics', 'ICT').

▪ A set of *learning objectives* for the whole unit, from which the learning objectives
for individual lessons can be drawn. In my example, these are called 'Learning
Challenges' and the 'Prime Learning Challenge'. Significant details can be drawn
from your unit map to help you form these learning objectives. You may want to
pick up on key words from the subject-related key concepts that have informed

Unit of Work	Spring Term	Year 3	2013/14
Area of Learning			
Learning Challenge 1			
Learning Challenge 2			
Learning Challenge 3			
Communication, Language and Literacy			
Mathematics			
ICT			
Physical Development			
PSE (SEAL)			
RE			
Trips, Visits, Visitors, Special Days			

Unit of Work	Spring Term		Year	2013/14
Prime Learning Challenge				
Subject Areas		Children's Prior Knowledge and Questions		
	Learning Challenges (Questions)	Knowledge, Skills and Understanding (NC)		Outcomes
Week 1				
Week 2				
Week 3				
Week 4				
Week 5				

Figure 7.4 Unit of work

your planning on the unit map, as well as the answers that you gave to the questions you defined within the unit map. Within my example unit of work document, key learning objectives also take the form of 'Learning Challenges (Questions)' within the context of individual lessons (that are outlined in a weekly list at the end of the form).

■ An indication of any *prior learning* that students should have achieved before commencing this particular unit of work. In my example, these are covered in the section titled 'Children's Prior Knowledge & Questions'.

■ An outline of how much *time* is available for the unit. This would include lesson time (i.e. how many lessons are within the unit, how long is each lesson and so on) as well as any homework time that might be assigned to the unit.

■ *Key resources* for the unit, including any specific pieces of information and communication technologies (ICT) that the unit might feature, any published resources that might be used, any artefacts or other objects that you will need access to, and key online resources (e.g. websites or other interactive resources) that you will need to utilise.

■ A simple description of any *assessment, personalisation or differentiation strategies* that will be used throughout the unit. These should be general, not specific to individual lessons, and should highlight any innovative approaches or specific assessment requirements (i.e. those related to the National Curriculum or examination specifications if appropriate).

■ A list of the *individual lessons* within the unit of work, together with one or two sentences describing each one, key knowledge and skills covered, and the expected outcomes. The unit of work should present an overview of these lessons (i.e. not detailed content) so that anyone reading the unit of work gets a general feel for the flow of lessons throughout the unit. Do keep this concise. This is not the time to write another bunch of lesson plans!

■ General statements related to the *other curriculum links* – for example, cross-curricular links, extension and enrichment strategies, future learning (i.e. what the unit of work leads into) and key vocabulary.

In the secondary school, units of work as described above are often written by heads of department for their curriculum team. It is common for individual teachers to be asked to complete a specific unit of work as part of their professional development. If you are working in a secondary school as the sole representative of that subject (e.g. a Drama or Music teacher), then you will get the job of doing all the planning yourself!

In the primary school, units of work are often written by teachers with a specific responsibility for a year group across the school. These responsibilities are normally shared across the staff in the school under the direction of the headteacher or a deputy headteacher with responsibility for the curriculum.

In either case, as an individual teacher working within a specific school, you may find yourself delivering a unit of work planned and written by someone else. It is important to remember that these documents are there to serve as a guide for your own individual lesson planning and subsequent teaching. There will be many different ways that a unit of work can be delivered depending on the nuance and style that you want to develop. How you plan your individual lessons in line with the unit of work plan will still depend on a range of factors, of which the general coverage provided by the unit of work is just one. So consider the unit of work as a map of the terrain rather than a specific guide of how you might navigate through that terrain. How you move the students from point A to point B is still your responsibility as their teacher! Do you remember the answer to question 6 in Chapter 1? Never teach from someone else's lesson plan.

All teachers are responsible for creating a sense of direction, purpose and flow between their lessons. This is a vital and important part of your pedagogy that you will need to practise. The unit of work document can help provide that formal framework for teaching but, as I have said, it will need some interpretation for use within lessons. There are a range of pedagogical strategies that you can utilise to develop this broader sense of flow across a unit of work including:

- The provision of summaries of learning through plenaries at key moments during your lessons.

- Highlighting or signposting future learning opportunities at the end of one lesson that created a sense of expectation and positive engagement in the students' minds for the next lesson.

- Using homework opportunities to establish links between lessons.

- Using virtual learning environments to engage with students' learning between lessons and across the school/home divide.

As with the lesson plan, the unit of work planning process is something that you will need to bring to life within your teaching. Otherwise, it will remain a paper exercise that is more a source of frustration than a positive element of your pedagogy.

The short-term plan: the lesson plan document

Although I have spent most of this book avoiding the presentation of a lesson plan document itself, the time has come to put forward a provisional lesson plan document that you could take and use in your teaching. As I have been at pains to emphasise throughout this book, there is no one magic bullet of a blank lesson plan document that will allow you to become the perfectly planned teacher! But, as we have seen, this is not to say that lesson plan documents are not helpful. A quick search of the Internet will reveal numerous approaches to lesson plan documents: some are very wordy, some have loads of pictures, some are based around PowerPoint presentations, others are done in cartoon form! Clearly, some teachers have a highly individualistic approach to this.

Before we consider the exemplar lesson plan document below, please take to heart the key message of this book. Spending excessive amounts of time on long, detailed plans will not automatically lead to better quality teaching on your part, or learning on your students' part. For once, I have found myself agreeing with something that Sir Michael Wilshaw, Her Majesty's Chief Inspector of Education, has said in relation to teachers who he has worked with:

> Planning was everything, but ... teachers were not slaves to their lesson plans. For each lesson, they would know what they were going to do, what resources they were going to deploy and roughly how long each activity

would take. But they also understood that planning should not be too detailed or too rigid. It was a framework and support, but they adapted what they did at key moments in the lesson, for example when something was not working or when the mood of the class changed. (RSA 2012)

However, it is also clear in my mind that a teacher who disengages with the cyclical process of planning, teaching and evaluating for too long will become a poorer teacher; for those of you starting out in teaching, commit to each stage of this process and you will improve your teaching immensely.

Figure 7.5 presents the lesson plan document from the PGCE course that I have worked on at the Faculty of Education at Manchester Metropolitan University since 2001. Over the years, this document has changed and developed in various ways but certain core elements have remained the same. We have used this document with hundreds of young teachers and, whilst I am not suggesting it is a perfect document, I would recommend it to you as something to try out at the start of your teaching career.

By now, many of the ingredients of this form will be instantly recognisable to you. But, for clarity, Table 7.1 contains a very quick breakdown of the form and the various details you will need to fill in.

I would strongly recommend this form as the starting point for your individual lesson planning.

Following on from this, there are a number of other more complex lesson planning forms that you could adopt and use within your teaching. Some of these will be presented to you within the particular school that you are working within (either as a student teacher or perhaps in your first teaching role). In either of these scenarios, all I would suggest is that you evaluate the lesson plan form you are given against the key elements contained in the above template. If anything is missing, you will need to ask yourself why. I would argue that all the above elements are essential for planning an individual lesson.

By way of a contrast, Figure 7.6 presents a much more detailed lesson planning form used by staff on the PGCE course at Birmingham City University. I am grateful to Professor Fautley and Dr Simon Spencer, course leaders for the PGCE, for allowing me to publish this template in this book.

I am not proposing to go through this template in the same detail as I did for Figure 7.5 as it already contains plenty of advice and examples in the explanatory text within the various sections.

My key point here is that you use these two examples (Figures 7.5 and 7.6) as a benchmark to judge the content of other lesson plan documents or templates that you will find in schools or online. Resist the urge to adopt simpler and shorter documents because you feel that they will give you an easier ride or result in quicker planning! In the early stages of learning to teach, taking shortcuts with your planning is a very bad idea and can have all kinds of negative consequences for yourself and your students.

Unit of Work: **Lesson Title:**

The Big Picture/Context

Learning Objectives

Learning Outcomes (knowledge, skills and understanding)

All pupils (working towards) will…

Most pupils (working at) will…

Some pupils (working beyond) will…

Inclusion and Extension Activities

Cross-Curricular Links

Assessment Strategies

Resources

Timings	Teaching Activity
	Starter activities
	Main Development activities/tasks
	Plenary activities

Homework

Lesson Evaluation

What were the <u>actual</u> learning outcomes for the lesson?
- *What did the pupils learn? How do I know?*
- *What went well? How do I know?*
- *What didn't go well? How do I know?*

Targets for next lesson:
- *What am I going to do about it? What will I change and/or retain: resources, room layout, activities?*

Figure 7.5 Lesson plan

Table 7.1 Lesson plan document items and their descriptions

Item	Description
Class	Add details of the class you are teaching.
Date	Add the date when the lesson is going to take place.
Unit of work	Add the title of the unit of work within which the lesson is located.
Lesson title	Add the title of the lesson (make it an interesting one!).
The big picture/context	Add a sentence here that describes the broader context within which this lesson is located. This could be copied across from the unit of work document description of the lesson. See Chapter 2 for further details.
Learning objectives	Write down your learning objectives for this specific lesson here. Remember, make the learning objectives describe the learning not the activities. And two or three learning objectives is fine (but no more). See Chapter 2 for further details.
Learning outcomes	Write your learning outcomes here. Remember, these could relate to the key knowledge, skills or understanding that you are expecting students to develop. Differentiate these in a simple way through the 'all, most and some' statements. See Chapter 2 for further details.
Inclusion and extension activities	Provide details here of how you are going to ensure that every student is included and challenged by the teaching activities contained within the lesson. In other words, these will be your strategies for differentiation and personalisation. See Chapter 6 for further details.
Cross-curricular links	Provide details here of any cross-curricular links that your lesson might be able to facilitate. See Chapter 8 for further details.
Assessment strategies	Provide a short statement here that outlines your key approaches towards the assessment of student learning throughout the lesson. Remember, this might involve students assessing their own and others' work. See Chapter 5 for further details.
Resources	List all the resources that you will need for the lesson. Use this as a checklist before the lesson starts. Be organised! See Chapter 4 for further details.
Timings	Add provisional timings for each part of the lesson. In the early days of your teaching, try to be precise here and stick to your timings if at all possible. As you get more experienced, you will begin to sense the flow of the lesson more intuitively. See Chapter 3 for further details.

Table 7.1 Continued

Item	Description
Teaching activity	This plan presents a simple three-part lesson (starter, main development task, plenary). This is a good place to start. However, there are other lesson structures that you can explore. Whatever structure you choose, outline the key stages of part of the lesson through short 'chunks'. In the early days of teaching, you may want to provide quite a bit of detail here. Later on, you can be more concise. See Chapter 3 for further details.
Homework	Add details of any homework tasks here (and do not forget to set it during the lesson). See Chapter 4 for further details.
Lesson evaluation	Rather than adopting a separate form for your evaluation, why not include it here underneath your lesson plan? See Chapter 9 for further details.

Planning in the primary and secondary school

Throughout this book I have dealt with lesson planning as a set of ideas and ways of thinking that can be applied equally within any educational setting, including primary, secondary, further education and higher education settings. However, I need to acknowledge that there are differences in the approach to planning within certain types of schools. For the key audience of this book, this will generally be primary and secondary schools. I suspect that as you have been reading this chapter, you have noticed that some of these have come to the fore. In my planning for this book, I have interviewed teachers from many different schools about their planning. This has been a tremendously helpful and interesting experience. During the course of these interviews, I have been struck by how many similarities there are between the planning processes of teachers working within the primary and the secondary school.

But I think it is self-evident that there are differences in approach to the organisation and delivery of education in these schools that casts an interesting light on how teaching and learning is planned. In the final part of this chapter I want to explore some of these and, by doing so, to help you think a little differently about how you go about planning lessons within the particular school context that you are working within. I will start with some of the most obvious differences between primary and secondary schools and work my way down into some of the finer details and how these impact on the discrete elements of lesson planning.

PGCE Secondary
Lesson Plan – Notes for Guidance and Examples

BIRMINGHAM
CITY
University

Section A – Information

Subject:		Date:		Time of Lesson:		Date:	
Unit of Work:		Class:		Number of Pupils:		Class:	

Title/Focus of Lesson: A separate lesson plan should be completed for each class, even if the body of the lesson has been taught already to a different group

Section B – Professional Development Links:

The following **Teachers' Standards** (Prompts) will be addressed:
2 or 3 Teachers Standards Prompts (sub-heading) is usual. Evidence from this lesson can be cross-referenced to the Professional Development Profile

Action Points from last lesson *(see section J of previous lesson plan)*:
After the first lesson, this information ensures the sequential nature of lessons where learning is developmental

Section C – Aims: *Select aims related to the Unit of Work (maximum 2)*

To provide opportunities for pupils to:
Aims need to link clearly to those from the unit of work to which this lesson refers. They should be limited to those that **will be** addressed **in this** lesson rather than a list of those for the entire unit.

Section D – Intended Learning: By the end of the lesson…

Differentiation for Groups: By the end of the lesson…

'Groups' (below) should be identified for this section and might include the gifted and talented (G&T), those with disabilities, Additional Learning Needs (ALN) or Special Educational Needs (SEN), Looked after children (LAC), English as an additional language (EAL), Free School Meals (FSM), Individual Education Plans (IEPs), Emotional and Behavioural Difficulties (EBD) and so on.

Pupils will have learned:
Statements of intended learning should indicate what the majority of pupils in the group are expected to achieve, not do. It is helpful to use the stem *'pupils will have learned that or how to…'*

Additional Challenge. These pupils will have learned:
Statements of intended learning in this section will be based on those to the left but will indicate additional learning challenges for the most able in the group.

Text to share with pupils related to intended learning:
Where required, this text will be based on the intended learning statements but couched in pupil-friendly terms. The school's customs and requirements regarding intended learning can also be included here.

Additional Support. These pupils will have learned:
Statements of intended learning in this section will be based on those above and left but will indicate learning for those in the group who require additional support. These pupils should also be appropriately challenged.

Figure 7.6 Exemplar lesson plan with detailed comments

This section will indicate how named pupils will have access to the lesson in terms of activities, content, assumed skills and use of equipment. Clear and specific notes are expected to indicate the action the teacher will take to support these pupils. Across a sequence of lessons a range of pupils should be considered, not only those with known or obvious needs. This section is very much concerned with individuals.

Section F – Resources Checklist:	**Section G – Homework / Independent Learning:**
A function list as an aide memoire.	This should be in line with the school policy and should be linked clearly to the lesson. Success or assessment criteria should be included as well as tasks and logistical arrangements.

Section H – Lesson Plan:

Time:	Learning:	Teaching:	Assessment:
	The intended learning for each activity, with clear links or reference to Section D, above.	The teaching activities and strategies, and pupil activities. This should include key points/concepts for explanations and modelling, and key questions for questions and discussions. Detailing pupil activities separate from teacher activities will help to ensure that the balance of the lessons is in favour of pupils' learning. The relationship between the activities here, the learning (left) and the assessment (right) should be clear. Logistical arrangements for assessment activities should be included here.	Provide the criteria that will determine the success of the activity. This is important even where the response may seem obvious. Stating the intended response and/or outcome is important to clarify expectations.
For example	That Birmingham is an industrialised city.	• Teacher models how to interrogate a picture using projection and writing key questions next to example picture; e.g. What does the picture show? Are there links between items? What are the implications of X, Y or Z? • Small groups interrogate pictures of B'ham City. Differentiated pictures used to scaffold responses and challenge the more able.	Pupils are able to identify buildings that pertain to industry and evidence of industrial activity. Most pupils draw conclusions beyond the picture – e.g. the canal was built to transport materials.

Figure 7.6 Continued

Class:	Class:	Class:

Section I – Assessment for Learning

What have some individual [named] pupils learned in relation to your stated learning outcomes?	*What is the evidence for this?*
Section I (4 parts) must be completed after each lesson, the sooner the better. For this reason, handwriting the response is perfectly acceptable. Mere description of the lesson is inadequate here, as are bland statements such as 'the pupils achieved all of the intended learning….' Responses need to reflect the extent to which intended learning was achieved and the quality of learning. The named pupils should include those highlighted in Sections D and E above. For example: It was clear that Hassan understood that Birmingham is an industrialised city, making a number of connections between key features.	This section is a continuation and is intended to foster analysis, not merely description; it may be preferable to treat these two sections as one. Specific examples or instances from the lessons should be cited to clarify evaluative judgements made about named pupils. For example: This was evidence from the annotations made in connection with the picture. Hassan cited two good examples of synthesising information to arrive at conclusions.
What additional, unexpected or unplanned outcomes were apparent in this lesson?	*What learning targets for some individual pupils need to be set?*
References to enjoyment or behaviour are only significant in terms of how they affect achievement and progress. For example: Most pupils had not interrogated a picture in such a structured manner before. This appeared very successful.	The emphasis here is on learning targets rather than behavioural targets. For example: Hassan could be challenged by considering the Birmingham map of 1870. Anna describes well but needs to talk through implications of what she has indentified.

Section J – Evidence of Reflective Practice: | Complete for _every_ lesson taught until Easter. Complete for one lesson per day after Easter

What aspects of the lesson were successful, and why?	*What are your action points for the next time you teach this group and/or lesson? (Transfer to the next lesson plan for this group/lesson)*
This needs to be objective and analytical; the what, how and why of the lesson. Strengths and achievements are also important and should be discussed. How pupils responded and reacted to the teaching might also be significant. For example: Teacher modelling worked very well using IWB because the pupils saw the whole process and had a clear idea of expectations.	Identifying significant features must lead to strategies to change, develop or refine practice. Analysis must lead to action! For this reason, the requirement to complete this section is relaxed after Easter. For example: Include greater challenge for Hassan. Place Anna with Salema for guided talking activity.

Figure 7.6 Continued

The organisation of students within the school

One of the most obvious differences between primary and secondary schools is the number of students that they cater for. A typical secondary school has around 1100 pupils; an average primary school around 200 pupils (DfE 2010). Although students are generally organised by age groups within both schools, the notion of a 'class' is very different in each setting. Primary school children are generally taught in one class group throughout each day; secondary school children, although placed in a form group, work in any number of different class groups depending on the curriculum arrangements and policies. The consequences of this on your work as a teacher are significant: a typical secondary school teacher will normally work with hundreds of different students each week; the primary school teacher will generally work with the same 25 to 35 students each day. Why not try to work this out in terms of the average time that each teacher will spend with any one student throughout a typical week? The results are massively different. As we have seen in the previous chapter, this has significant impact on all aspects of planning including the ability to differentiate effectively for individual pupils.

The curriculum arrangements within the school

A second very important difference between primary and secondary schools is the structure of the curriculum arrangements that teachers have to work under. The overarching curriculum structures for the Early Years, Key Stages 1 and 2 are different from those at Key Stages 3 and the GCSE and GCE examination specifications that frame teachers' work at Key Stages 4 and 5. These impact on the way that an individual subject is located within the curriculum and the consequent impact of this on staffing, subject expertise and planning are considerable.

For example, in the primary school, key subject areas such as literacy, numeracy and science are often planned for and taught as specific areas; however, other foundation subjects are planned for and taught within topic areas (as we discussed earlier in this chapter). In the average secondary school, the vast majority of lessons are taught in subject areas, with only occasional topic-based or cross-curricular approaches being utilised for specific days or events.

From the perspective of the student at a secondary school, the organisation of the school, in its physical layout, staffing and curriculum organisation, serves to differentiate between subjects in a very rigid way. History is taught in one place by Mr Smith; Mathematics is taught in another place by Miss Choke; Design and Technology is taught in the workshop by Mrs Philpot, and so on. Whilst the curriculum frameworks that have resulted in this division are perhaps understandable, it is important to remember that from a students' perspective this is a massive shift in how they experience the processes of teaching and learning in comparison to what they experienced throughout their primary education.

The organisation of teachers within the school

Another large difference between primary and secondary schools is what is often characterised as a division between generalist and specialist teachers. For a range of historical, societal and cultural reasons, and put simply, many primary school teachers are generalists, being able to teach many different subjects to their class throughout the week. Although many primary school teachers may have a particular subject specialism (perhaps something that they have studied to degree level or beyond), the vast majority of them work in a generalist capacity. In some larger primary schools there may be subject specialist teachers but this is fairly uncommon. In contrast, secondary school teachers are characterised as subject specialists, teaching the same subject to multiple classes throughout the course of any given week.

These divisions are enforced through the ways in which universities educate teachers. The vast majority of primary school teachers are educated through a three-year undergraduate route leading to qualified teacher status (QTS). There are no undergraduate routes leading to QTS for secondary school teaching. Until recently, every secondary school teacher will have done a subject degree followed by a PGCE or a one-year course leading to QTS.

The balance between an in-depth subject specialism obtained through studying for a specific degree and a more generalist approach to subject content of the kind that you might get on an undergraduate course in primary education can be both a strength and a weakness. Primary school teachers are experts in planning content from multiple subject areas in innovative combinations through sophisticated models of cross-curricular teaching and learning. The 'average' secondary school teacher can have an impressive knowledge of their subject area, but this can also be constrained by the notion of their 'subject' and how it is perceived and organised within the structure of the school and the various curriculum frameworks within which they work. As an example, the Key Stage 4 GCSE specifications will outline, in detail, exact areas of subject content that need to be covered within a programme of study during Years 10 and 11. Some teachers will find the opportunity to devise innovative topic-based approaches within this programme limiting (although I have noted that this does not stop some teachers innovating in these areas in spite of what other teachers see as 'impositions' or 'restrictions' on their work).

For all these reasons, and probably many more, the processes of planning a lesson do need to be reflected on within the specific context within which that lesson has taken place. This book has attempted to outline the key stages of lesson planning in a general way. The way in which you adopt and adapt these processes will have to be done in an individual way that reflects who you are as a teacher as well as the school that you are teaching within.

Summary

In this chapter I have explored a range of approaches to the documentation and planning of learning. We began with the curriculum overview map that provides a simple way to document the longer-term processes of planning across a key stage. From there, we considered the unit of work map which I presented as a medium-term plan, spanning across the work of a term or half a term and providing an interim perspective on the teaching and learning that will occur.

Finally, and perhaps most importantly for this book, we considered the lesson plan template itself. Whilst the two templates that I have included in this chapter are not perfect, they do represent a useful starting point for your work in planning lessons in the primary or secondary school.

I have emphasised that it is important to recognise that the context within which you are working (be it a primary school, secondary school or somewhere else) will shape the planning and teaching that you undertake. But the general stages of lesson planning that I have presented throughout this book are applicable to both and will provide you with an excellent starting point for your own lesson planning.

In the following two chapters, we will turn our attention to the remaining two vital elements of becoming a brilliant teacher: the performance of the lesson itself and the evaluation of teaching and learning.

References

DfE (2010) Schools, pupils and their characteristics: January 2010. www.education.gov.uk/researchandstatistics/statistics/a00196394/ (accessed 21 November 2013).

RSA (2012) The good teacher. www.thersa.org/fellowship/journal/archive/summer-2012/features/the-good-teacher (accessed 10 December 2013).

8 The 'performance' of teaching

Introduction

The vast majority of this book has been about lesson planning. Starting with the identification and formation of learning objectives and outcomes, the design of engaging teaching activities, the selection of quality resources and techniques of assessment, differentiation and personalisation, I have led you through what I consider are the key issues in forming a good lesson plan. But in one very important sense, all that planning and preparation that you can do for an individual lesson, or sequence of lessons, means very little if you cannot bring that plan to life through the actual act of teaching. For this reason, throughout the book I have been urging you to think about your pedagogy, the actual art and craft of teaching, through a range of practical and other activities.

One of the key messages of this book is that the time you spend lesson planning is not wasted time. Done properly, it will have important consequences for your actions within the classroom. This is particularly true in the early part of your teaching career. Whilst I have been writing this book I have been visiting my own students who are undertaking their very first teaching practice placements. They have been teaching whole classes for a couple of weeks. In my meetings with them it is not uncommon for me to ask how long they are taking in planning an individual lesson. For many, it does take a long time at first. With practice, of course, this time will shorten. But there are vital links between planning, teaching and evaluation (which I will consider further in my final chapter) that you need to deliberately foster and develop. This triangle of activity underpins the vast majority of your work as a teacher. The most important point is to make explicit and constructive links between the time you spend planning lessons, the time you spend actually teaching and the time you spend evaluating your work. Within this chapter, I am going to explore this triangle in some detail and encourage you to make constructive links between these three key activities.

Defining what we mean by pedagogy

What do you think of when you hear the word 'pedagogy'? How would you define it? How do you describe the physical act of teaching? What does it involve? An obvious response would be that it involves you doing things – speaking, listening, moving, describing, explaining, assessing, analysing – and these things involve both your mind and your body. But when you try to pin down precisely what constitutes an effective pedagogy, it is perhaps a little bit more tricky. It is not something that is easily observed. Although specific things might be noted, they work together in a way that is often difficult to diagnose. For this reason, it can seem that skilful and experienced teachers are able to teach with apparent ease and with an elusive quality. As a young teacher, perhaps you have had to watch lessons delivered by more experienced teachers prior to doing some teaching yourself; maybe you are watching the exact lesson that you know you are going to have to teach in a few days' time. No doubt you have done this conscientiously and perhaps you have made notes or even engaged in a discussion with the teacher following the lesson to find out why they did the things that they did. Why did they talk to that student in that particular way? Why did they move to that point in the room at that particular moment? What was going on in their mind when they deviated from their lesson plan to spend a bit more time questioning that student about their work? But when the time comes to teach your lesson, despite your best planning and preparation, the delivery of the lesson does not seem to be quite so smooth, the flow is a little more disjointed and, perhaps, the learning that the students engaged with is not so intense. Why? After all, didn't you do everything the same as the teacher you observed?

The reason is simple. Planning and preparation for a lesson is important and builds on skills that you can learn relatively quickly. We have discussed the vast majority of them within the space of this short book. But developing a skilful, practical, pedagogy takes time; it is something that can engage you for a whole career – a lifetime perhaps! Experienced teachers are able to draw on years of practice and can make teaching look very easy. In order to help get to that point yourself, my advice is to commit to the three key and interrelated processes of planning, teaching and reflection. Make the development of this skilful pedagogy your number one priority in the first few years of your teaching. But in order for your classroom practice to improve, you must do the other two elements. Good teaching will not develop or emerge by accident. It has to be planned for. In order for this to be sustained, it must be reflected on conscientiously so that key lessons are identified and reinforced systematically. But I am getting ahead of myself. In order to do any of this, you need to settle in your mind a few foundational principles. What, exactly, is pedagogy and how can you develop it?

One of the most influential figures in discussions surrounding pedagogy has been Professor Robin Alexander. As a Fellow of Wolfson College at the University of Cambridge and Director of the Cambridge Primary Review, Alexander defines pedagogy as:

> the act of teaching together with its attendant discourse. It is what one needs to know, and the skills one needs to command, in order to make and justify the many different kinds of decisions of which teaching is constituted. (Alexander 2008, p. 11)

Alexander makes the key point that pedagogy is not the same as teaching. Pedagogy involves teaching but it is much more than teaching alone. It involves an 'attendant discourse' that comprises the knowledge and skills which inform, justify and value the decision-making processes within teaching. Pedagogy is both a 'practice' and a 'process' through which certain ways of thinking can be acquired or through which certain actions can be developed, justified and valued.

Skilful teachers embody a skilful pedagogy. It is part of their 'being' as a teacher. This is important because you cannot 'be' another teacher. You have to find and develop your teaching identity for yourself. Other teachers are responsible for the development and application of their pedagogy; you will be responsible for yours – but it will look, sound and feel different. This skilful pedagogy does not appear by accident. It develops over a long period of time and needs constant nurturing through carefully planning, critically analysing, reflecting on and evaluating your work. Pedagogy is all the various elements of your thinking, planning and preparation that you do prior to a lesson, together with all the intellectual, physical and emotional aspects of delivering the lesson, as well as the processes of reflection and evaluation that you will undertake after the lesson has been delivered. In short, it is everything that you need to 'be' in order to be a teacher.

Throughout the previous seven chapters of this book we have considered all the aspects that you will need to develop in order to plan an effective lesson, or series of lessons. In this chapter, our attention turns to your performance in the classroom. However, it is important not to leave the combined impact of the previous chapters behind. All the lessons contained in those chapters will be relevant here. You cannot have one without the other. I have laboured this point in the introduction to this chapter because it is vitally important. I hope that this important conceptual and practical point will be illustrated in what follows. I want to explore it further by reference to a key conceptual framework (drawn from Alexander's work) and through a range of 'performance' metaphors.

Making connections through your teaching: the dialogic curriculum

Different writers have expressed the link between planning and pedagogy in a range of ways. One approach that I have found helpful is Alexander's definition of the 'dialogic curriculum'. By 'dialogic', Alexander does not solely mean dialogue (although, of course, we all know that dialogue is a massive part of teaching);

dialogic, for Alexander, is an interpretation of the work of Mikhail Bakhtin and encompasses:

> the interaction of minds and ideas as well as words, that transcends the boundaries of time, space and culture, that entails imagination, empathy and the making of connections, and that may even be one of the keys to our survival as a species. (Alexander 2008, p. 138)

In a fundamental way, pedagogy, for Alexander, is about making these types of connections. The most important connection is the one between you, as a teacher, and your students. Have you ever paused to consider what this actually means? For me, teaching is one of the most important jobs that anyone can do. Through teaching, we are shaping the lives of our students in important ways. At parties or other social events, I expect that you are often asked, 'What do you do?' How do you respond? Perhaps you say, 'Oh, I'm just a teacher.' I hope not. Please do not downplay the importance of teaching in this way. Perhaps you say, 'I'm a teacher at . . .' This is probably followed by a question such as, 'What do you teach?' At this point, the situation can get interesting. What do you actually teach? For those of you working in secondary schools, perhaps you say that you are a teacher of English, Mathematics or whatever your subject specialism is; for primary teachers, perhaps you say that you are teaching Year 3 or 4, and so on. Of course, at one level, this is entirely correct. But at a deeper level, teachers do not just teach a subject or a year group. You teach life itself. In a philosophical sense, you teach yourself.

The connections that you make with students are more fundamental than those provided by an individual subject or a curriculum framework. Teaching is a human activity. In times past, teachers used to talk about the 'hidden curriculum'. What did they mean by this? At a simple level, it meant everything that the school environment taught students that could not be easily written down. It was about how humans react to each other, how they behave together, how to develop sympathy and empathy in our interactions, how to value, nurture and support each other through hard times and much more.

I learnt this lesson the hard way. As a young teacher, I remember watching a teacher teaching a class at the beginning of the school day. The teacher was experienced but several students in the class were misbehaving at the opening of the lesson. However, she did not seem to be dealing with their behaviour in a rigorous way. I remember writing down some notes to that effect in my journal. With the arrogance of youth, I felt that the teacher was not clamping down strongly enough on those students and that given the opportunity I would do things differently. Following the lesson, I was keen to ask the teacher about why she dealt with those students in the way that she did. When I did ask her, she paused and sighed. She started to tell me about each of their lives outside of the school environment. By the time she had finished, my thoughts had sobered considerably. Given everything they were coping with, it was a minor miracle that they had even made it into school on time and eventually engaged with the lesson in the way that they did. The misbehaviour at the beginning of the lesson, when seen in the context of their broader lives, was forgivable.

I mention this story at this point because it was humbling for me. It taught me an important lesson. The lesson was not that we should ignore students' poor behaviour or excuse it. Rather, it was that teaching is based on human interactions that deals with students who have real and sometimes difficult lives, but who need and deserve to be engaged with, cared for and taught as individuals. All our students have names (so let's use them), have moments in their lives of great joy and sadness that they will want to share (so let's find out a bit about their lives outside of school), have families and other significant people in their lives (with all that this entails so let's engage with some of that) and much, much more besides. They are children who need to be nurtured and cared for by teachers who understand them and view them as such (not as numbers on a spreadsheet who need to be moved from Level 5c to Level 5a in the next academic year).

Those last four paragraphs might have sounded like a bit of a rant (and we have definitely strayed a little off the dialogic curriculum pathway!), but I wanted to emphasise, again, that teaching is based on a human relationship within which important connections are made. Actually, it is not too far from Alexander's thinking to which we ought to return.

In his fascinating book, Alexander explores what a 'dialogic curriculum' might look like through five starting points:

1 Realms of knowledge and ways of knowing

2 Generic skills

3 Forms of intelligence

4 Ways of learning

5 Hybrids.

These starting points present an interesting way in for our discussion about how planning and pedagogy are inextricably linked. They provide different departure points for the types of 'connections' that you will want to make with your students. For, as any performer knows, a good performance needs to be planned for in considerable detail and, most importantly, the performer has to have an idea of what they are wanting to communicate to their audience. As the teacher, you will be responsible for initiating the conversation, reaching out and beginning to make those all important connections.

Connection point 1: realms of knowledge and ways of knowing

In Alexander's dialogic pedagogy, realms of knowledge and ways of knowing go far beyond mere bodies of information. For him, they are 'distinct ways of knowing, understanding, enquiring and making sense' (ibid., p. 140) that include many key processes of enquiry, modes of explanation and criteria for verification. Used skilfully, these dimensions will not only equip students with a knowledge and understanding of a specific subject, but will also provide a set of essential tools that are applicable into other domains too. Your first vitally important connection point as a teacher will be to initiate students into these realms rather than just transmitting information about them.

Alexander believes that knowledge-based curricula have received a bad press in recent years precisely because they often result in a pedagogical approach that is stifling and disengaging. It is:

> associated with transmissive, monologic teaching by rote, recitation or exposition, which too often destroys what it is supposed to arouse: the excitement of knowing and understanding. It is schooling that has reduced knowledge to 'subjects' and teaching to mere 'telling'. (Ibid., p. 141)

But this need not be the case. As we will go on to see, there are pedagogical approaches that can recapture the excitement of, and engagement with, realms of knowledge and ways of knowing. The planning that you do for a lesson needs to find the tools by which you can introduce and connect students to these new areas; your skilful pedagogy will transport them there.

Connection point 2: generic skills

Drawing on Alexander's concept of a dialogic curriculum, the second key connection point that you will want to develop through your pedagogy relates to generic skills. The generic skills that our students need to develop through their educational experiences are many and varied. Lists of these skills tend to include items such as:

- Leadership
- Teamwork
- Social and interpersonal skills
- Communication
- Enterprise
- Research
- Thinking
- Problem-solving.

And I could continue for some time!

At the level of curriculum development, for many teachers and schools generic skills are contrasted with knowledge. For these educators, generic skills become the antidote to subjects because they combine relevance, perhaps to the workplace and employability, with the hands-on experiences that students are demanding. This type of approach has some significant consequences for your lesson planning and may encourage you to consider generic skills of this type in isolation from the realms of knowledge and ways of knowing that we considered in connection point 1.

Alexander's dialogic pedagogy questions this approach. If generic skills, he argues, are *all* that a curriculum offers, then we are in a difficult place. For him, a generic skills approach:

> Sells such [lifelong] learning short, for it elevates being able to do something over knowing, understanding, reflecting, speculating, analysing and evaluating, which arguably are no less essential to the fulfilled, successful and useful life. Indeed, without these capacities, the exercise of skill becomes, in a very real sense, meaningless. (Ibid., p. 143)

There is a tendency in our contemporary educational discourse to consider all aspects of learning within this umbrella term of 'skills'. But this eliminates essential distinctions between knowing, understanding and doing that can have some dire consequences for the quality of educational experiences that we offer to our students. In developing connection point 2 you will want to consider how knowledge, ways of knowing and skills can all be presented and modelled within your pedagogy in order for them to meaningfully impact on your students. It is not good enough to just tell students about something and not do it or exemplify it yourself. As teachers, we need to walk the walk and not just talk the talk!

Connection point 3: recognising different forms of intelligence

What is intelligence? Is it possible to measure how intelligent a student is? As a teacher, are you able to tell which students are more intelligent than other students? Despite what Boris Johnson says (Wintour 2013), previous ways of thinking about intelligence as a fixed entity, measurable by testing to produce an intelligence quotient (IQ), have begun to give way to two claims. First, intelligence may not be fixed but could be, instead, environmentally responsive; second, that intelligence is multiple rather than singular.

Alexander discusses the work of the most celebrated theorist of multiple intelligence – Howard Gardner (1999). His thinking was that there are eight 'multiple' intelligences (together with a possible ninth intelligence). These intelligences are:

- Linguistic

- Logico-mathematical

- Spatial

- Musical

■ Bodily-kinaesthetic

■ Interpersonal (how one relates to others)

■ Intrapersonal (how one understands oneself)

■ Naturalist (how one understands the observable world)

■ Existential (how one understands one's existence and place in the world).

In some schools, managers and teachers have become preoccupied with categorisations of student intelligence in a most unhelpful way. At the end of the day, whether a student has a single intelligence or a blend of different intelligences, the result is pretty immaterial for the ways in which you seek to connect with these students. Simply scoring students against criterion or an intelligence quotient is not going to help you in either your planning or pedagogical approach in and of itself.

Rather, Alexander comments that there are significant overlaps between this categorisation of intelligence and the typical, generic approach to the knowledge-based curriculum (such as those explored by Phenix (1964) or Hirst (1965)). Whether or not Gardner's theories are right or not is immaterial. Your pedagogical approach needs to demonstrate an approach to education that connects different ways of knowing and understanding at the centre of a pedagogy that helps students make sense of their world in an intelligent way.

Connection point 4: recognising different ways of learning

Similar arguments to those made above in respect of different 'forms' of intelligence can be made in respect of Alexander's fourth starting point for a dialogic approach to teaching and learning. Here, he returns to the work of Jerome Bruner whom, he acknowledges, was central to his thinking about a dialogic curriculum. Specifically, he draws on Bruner's definition of four 'folk pedagogies' in which students are perceived as being in various different forms of relationship to learning and knowledge:

■ Children as *imitators*: learning from modelling (which in its vocational or professional form becomes apprenticeship).

■ Children as *recipients*: learning by didactic exposure to propositional knowledge, or learning by telling; with knowledge viewed as being independent of the knower.

■ Children as *thinkers*: learning by intersubjective interchange and collaboration; with knowledge being seen as co-constructed.

■ Children as *knowledgeable*: learning by exploring the relationship between what is known personally and what is known canonically (i.e. from the culturally evolved realms of knowledge discussed above). (After Bruner 1996, pp. 53–62.)

Alexander agrees with Bruner that all four 'ways of learning' have their place (Alexander 2008, p. 146). These folk pedagogies give him the opportunity to define in a little more detail exactly who or what the 'dialogue' or dialogic education is between. As well as exchanges between teacher and student:

> The kinds of interaction between teacher and student that characterise dialogic teaching presuppose dialogue at [these] other levels too: between 'I' and 'me', between self and the outside world, between subjective and culturally given knowledge, between different ways of knowing and understanding, and between past, present and future. (Ibid., p. 147)

These forms of connections or interactions between yourself and your students are particularly rich and worth exploring further in your own pedagogy. They contrast strongly with other, weaker forms of 'learning styles' such as the visual, auditory and kinaesthetic approaches that have dominated many recent educational reforms, which I would encourage you to avoid at all costs as they seem to be particularly divisive in all kinds of ways. Please remember that neither Alexander, Bruner nor I are suggesting the students will naturally fit into one of the above four folk pedagogies. They will move between and around these categories depending on a whole host of variable factors. This is one reason why teaching is better thought of as artistry rather than as a science. It depends on the teacher being open to and responsive to the changing nature of their students. You should avoid rigid demarcations of students through forced categorisations at all costs.

Connection point 5: a hybrid approach to curriculum development

Hybrid approaches to education and curriculum combine elements of the above into particular models for schools to work within. Alexander cites three approaches in his chapter (ibid., pp. 148–9), of which Wragg's cubic curriculum (1997) is perhaps the most relevant to our discussion. This comprises ten subjects (English, Mathematics, Science and so on), eight cross-curricular issues (citizenship, linguistics and so on) and six teaching/learning styles (tell, discover, practise and so on). This hybrid approach reinforces the view that teaching well is a skilful mix of various forms of connection and engagement. Effective teaching and learning is not facilitated by a narrow or rigid perspective that positions students within fixed boundaries. As we saw in the previous chapter, we must build our planning and pedagogy on our understanding of them as unique human beings and start connecting with them as people not as numbers on a spreadsheet.

For you, the important point to remember is that these connection points will meld together into a skilful pedagogy given an appropriate conscientious approach to planning, a deliberate and sustained practice of a pedagogy that seeks to build on this planning, and a committed approach to evaluation (of which more in the next chapter) that seeks to monitor student engagement in a sustained way alongside reflections of your own teaching.

PRACTICAL TASK

Take each connection point above in turn and apply it to your work as a teacher. What are the practical implications of considering your teaching in terms of this dialogic model? What difference will it actually make to a lesson you are going to plan and teach? Try to identify a couple of specific practical outcomes and try something to form a new type of connection with your students in the next lesson that you teach.

In the opening part of the chapter we have explored together a famous curriculum model (the dialogic curriculum) and drawn inferences from this to help form a view that planning and pedagogy should work hand in hand. In the next key section of this chapter, I am going to focus on you and your pedagogy in the classroom. How does that lesson planning that you have done in private turn into a powerful and meaningful *performance of teaching* that will inspire your students to learn?

The performance of teaching

Lesson planning is normally a solitary, private activity that invokes many skills, including (but not limited to):

- Diagnosing and setting appropriate learning objectives

- Choosing relevant and purposeful teaching activities

- Designing assessment and differentiation frameworks

- Assembling or producing helpful resources

- And much more besides.

This private process comes to life within your classroom. Whilst not many students will ever ask to see your lesson plan, you, the teacher, will embody that lesson plan and present it to your students through your whole 'performance' during a specific lesson. Your pedagogy is the vehicle by which this embodiment and transformation can take place. For this reason, numerous educational thinkers, researchers and writers over the decades have emphasised the importance of the teacher in the process of curriculum development and delivery. This led Lawrence Stenhouse, a Professor of Education at the University of East Anglia, to famously state that there is 'no curriculum development without teacher development' (Stenhouse 1975).

This 'embodiment' of the curriculum in your pedagogy is worth pausing to consider in a little more detail. What is it that you are 'embodying'? In a very real sense you are embodying key aspects of all five of the connection points that we discussed above. First, these include important general 'ways of being' that students will learn to watch over time and learn from. These will include models of behaviour, communication and collaboration that you demonstrate in your dealings with students, other staff, parents, the caretaker and cleaners, and others; it will also include your seriousness in promoting active engagement in teaching and learning within your classroom. Second, in a more specific way, whether you are teaching in a primary or secondary school, you are the vital first point of contact in relation to the specific subjects (realms of knowledge) that you teach your pupils. For secondary school teachers, the science curriculum documentation may be in place but you, as a teacher of science, represent that subject – day in, day out – for your students. Like it or not, you 'live' science for them by the way that you act and behave as a teacher and scientist in your classroom. This has significant consequences for the way that you will teach science. If you are bored by your subject, can you really expect your students to be interested and engaged in it?

The same is true for primary school teachers. As you will have to teach a broader range of subjects and topics than your secondary colleagues, you need to be a passionate advocate for all the subjects that you teach, whether or not you feel that you are a specialist in that particular area. You will need to draw connections between them and show your students how an active and positive engagement with a broad range of knowledge, skills and understanding can result in a happy and fulfilled life. In this sense, students really do take the lead from you. If you want them to be enthusiastic, be enthusiastic yourself; if you want them to be engaged and motivated to learn, then you have to lead by example and provide that earnest and serious approach to support their learning that they deserve.

Stenhouse's key phrase teaches us that if we are serious about our intention to develop the curriculum that we offer to our pupils in this way, we cannot but help develop ourselves as teachers too. The two things work together in an intimate way. You will need to personalise this process in order to really understand the consequences of what it entails for your lesson planning. How do you *feel* about the lesson plan that you are putting together? Does it capture your imagination? Does it excite and inspire you as a teacher? If it does not, can you really expect it to inspire your students? Are you finding it hard to make natural links between the various sections of the lesson? Is the narrative of the lesson clearly identifiable? Does the lesson have a clear beginning, middle and end? If the answer to any of these questions is no, then it is probably unrealistic to expect the majority of your students to engage with and make sense of your lesson either.

But the way in which we, as teachers, embody the curriculum that we offer our students has other dimensions too. In recent years, government ministers have asked a number of challenging questions about what constitutes the act of teaching and who is qualified to undertake this role. Is knowledge of a subject alone enough to make an effective teacher? I would argue that it is not. Should teachers have a degree as a minimum qualification? I would argue that they should. Is teaching a craft? Without wanting to denigrate the word 'craft' in any way, I would argue that it is more than a craft and, at its best, can become an art. Is teaching a science? That's an interesting question! It takes us to the first of four metaphors that I want to briefly explore around this theme of the performance of teaching.

Teaching as science?

In their definitions of 'pedagogy', most dictionaries define the word as 'the science of teaching'. Do you think it is helpful to describe pedagogy as a science? Like any metaphor, there are going to be benefits as well as limitations of such a conception. On the plus side, science implies a clear process of enquiry. Doing 'good' science relies on defining key principles, utilising appropriate methods, carefully handling materials, being precise and rigorous. All these things could be considered as being part of a good pedagogical approach too. Additionally, planning is a central component of 'doing' good science. Do you remember practical science lessons where experiments were modelled by the teacher at the front of the classroom before you did them on benches around the laboratory? A key element of this approach is the experiment 'method', which has to be written up clearly and concisely as part of an account of the experiment. Recently, I had to go to my son's Year 8 parents' evening. He likes science and I spoke with his science teacher, who was generally complementary about his work. Unfortunately, for him, the one down side of his work was that he rushed the writing up stage of the work. To be honest, I remember doing the same. In science, it is not enough to merely find out the correct answer to a particular scientific problem. The process by which you have come to find out that answer has to be represented and accounted for in order for others to replicate that experiment and test your findings. Being able to write this process down in clear steps was an important part of 'doing' science well. This rule applies for Year 8 boys in exactly the same way as it would apply to someone wanting to publish a scientific study in an academic journal.

But as with any metaphors, there are limits to the idea of teaching being a science. As we explored through this chapter, it is often not possible to find the perfect mix of pedagogical ingredients and then combine them in the desired quantities, according to a particular method, and – hey presto – you become a perfect teacher! As I emphasised at the beginning of this chapter, teaching is built on human relationships and these do not lend themselves to be easily reducible to basic component parts. That said though, there is merit in the rigorous exploration of the specific elements or characteristics of a pedagogical approach through a simple process of planning, teaching and reflection. Finding ways of accounting for this in the 'method' of pedagogical enquiry would be a useful exercise at this early stage of your career. It might involve you doing a detailed and focused observation of a particular element of a teacher's pedagogy. For example, you might focus on a teacher's body language throughout part of a lesson and ask the following questions:

- Where do they stand/sit? (Plot their movement through a diagrammatic chart that represents their movement throughout the lesson.)

▓ What posture do they adopt (describe it in detail) and how does this flow from one posture to another?

▓ How do they use their hands to emphasise key points (when does this happen and how does it relate to the language they are using and the tone of their voice)?

▓ What barriers are there which inhibit their body language and can these be removed?

If you are feeling really brave, perhaps you could ask a colleague to make a video of you teaching and then analyse your own performance in this way.

Or, to provide another example, you might focus on the technique of explaining a new concept:

▓ How is the explanation structured (does it have one)?

▓ How does it relate to the key learning objectives that have been established within the lesson?

▓ What hooks are used to engage the pupils' curiosity (and are these an aide memoire for students later on)?

▓ How are key points repeated or re-emphasised throughout the explanation?

▓ What scaffolding devices are used? Are references made to existing knowledge structures and, if so, how are these extended?

▓ What, if any, links are there to modelling and how does this relate to any explanations that are given?

▓ How are the learning outcomes for the lesson highlighted or hinted at through the explanation and/or model?

This kind of detailed, almost forensic, analysis of a specific pedagogical technique or device can produce very rich learning experiences. However, as I emphasised above, just conducting the observation and finding out the 'correct' answer to your enquiry will not automatically translate into your being able to adopt an appropriate body language in the classroom, or explain new concepts better. Defining pedagogy as 'science of teaching' has its limitations.

So, alongside this first metaphor of 'teaching as science', I would like to bring a range of other metaphors into this debate. The next two of these relate teaching to a type of performance: first acting and second musicianship. Like teaching, the work that actors and musicians do in a performance builds on a specific set of skills and techniques, various pieces of knowledge and a broad understanding of the art form or music they are working within. Like teaching, these skilful players also engage in planning and preparation (they might call it 'rehearsal') that is often done in private and prior to a performance. I will start with the world of the theatre and the work of actors.

Teaching as acting

The theatre is a space that allows actors and audiences to dream together, to be taken to new places, to enjoy and be challenged by new experiences, and, at times, to think the unthinkable. One of the aspirations of any theatre production is that the audience will leave the theatre changed in some way as a result of experiencing the specific production. This has many similarities to the processes of teaching and learning in the classroom. As teachers, I am sure we could all agree that we hope that our students do not leave our classrooms in the same state that they entered them! Learning should have occurred and this, over time, will result in our students' cognitive and physical development. It should also result in us improving our pedagogy.

With the exception of the most improvisatory forms of theatre (of which more below), most actors work with a script that is written and prepared by someone else. In the majority of cases this script is fixed and cannot be altered. It contains the words and other directions needed to perform the play according to the desire of the author. In many theatre traditions – for example, Shakespearian – it would not be considered appropriate to change the words of the play although, of course, many other aspects – such as the context within which the play is set, the staging of the play, the lighting and sound design – could all be developed in ways far from those imagined by the original playwright (indeed, this is one of many aspects of producing a play that is in and of itself a highly creative and interpretive act).

However, it is worth pausing and considering whether or not the script, which the actors have to remember and deliver using all their performance skills, is really 'the play' in its entirety. As I have already mentioned, the words of the script as penned by the author are just one element of the performance that is framed by all kinds of other devices and structures. These would include the larger aspects of artistic direction such as a broader context for the play, the set and sound design, but it would also include elements that are intrinsic to the skills, techniques and work of an individual actor within this framework: the sound of their voice, the pace of their delivery, the emotional input that they impose onto the language, the way that they interact with other actors, and much more besides. I remember a recent production at the Royal Shakespeare Company (RSC) at which David Tennant played a leading role. At the time, he was also playing the role of Dr Who in the famous BBC programme of the same name. His presence as a leading actor in the production attracted an entirely new audience to the RSC partly due to his celebrity status but also because of his recognised talents as a Shakespearian actor.

But beyond all of these considerations are the audience themselves, who constitute another layer of interaction with which the actor needs to communicate. How they respond to the events that unfold before them has an intrinsic effect on what any individual actor may do. They may 'play to the house' during one performance in a way that they would not do on another occasion. In this sense, the play is different in every performance even though at a basic level certain elements such as the set design and costumes are likely to be fixed and unchangeable despite what an audience might think about them.

To what extent is this theatrical performance like the process of planning for teaching? At a basic level, you could compare the lesson plan document to a script. It contains the words, phrases, key sequences, questions and instructions needed to deliver a lesson. The teacher plays the role of the actor and the classroom becomes the set, the context for the performance that does play a fundamental role in bringing it to life (or not). Finally, of course, the students are the audience, invited into this space for a particular performance and engaged and changed, we hope, as a result.

But the metaphor begins to fall apart because it places the teacher in the dual role of author and actor. Initially, the lesson plan has to be imagined and created. It is written by the teacher (author) with a specific group of students in mind, for a specific place (their classroom) at a particular time (Tuesday morning, period 1). As we have seen, all of these aspects (students, place and time) need to be considered carefully and the plan needs to reflect that level of specific thinking. It will present a set of ideas through a narrative that has structure (some kind of scene setting leading to the main events of the play), key ideas (characters or topics) and some kind of resolution within a set time period. But, second, the teacher is also the actor charged with bringing the script to life within a specific performance event (the lesson). Here, like the actor, they have to bring all their human qualities and attributes to bear in order for the performance to be engaging and convincing.

With the teacher in the role of author and actor, perhaps an improvisatory approach provides a better model for the work of the teacher as a performer. But, rather than explore this idea within the context of the theatre, I will consider teaching as an alternative type of performance – a musical one – as we move to our third metaphor.

Teaching as musicianship

The third metaphor that I am going to reflect on here is that of musical performance, and in particular the work of the improvising musician. Like the actor, a musician is often required to work with a script (they would call it the 'score') that has been produced by a composer. Many of the considerations that we gave to the work of the actor apply equally to the musician. The score is the basis for a performance; however, it does not contain everything that is needed in order to give a convincing performance. Like the actor's script, the musician's score has to be interpreted in light of a number of factors.

These factors are informed by the musician's understanding of the specific performance conventions that surround the period of time when the music was written or the style that it exhibits. So, for example, a musical score from the Baroque period of music (e.g. the work of Vivaldi) would need to be approached in a different way to a score produced by a Romantic composer such as Brahms. Part of this is because of the amount of detail that such a score may or may not contain. There is a general movement in the history of music for scores to contain more and more detail within them as they get closer to the present day. For example, Vivaldi might have been quite happy to tell his musicians to play quietly or loudly; Brahms' scores contain very precise instructions about the volume of specific passages of music within his score, as well as the gradual changes of volume that might occur over a period of time. The same is true of many other aspects of music's composition and performance. By the twentieth century, the musical score itself had become a very detailed representation of the composer's wishes that the performing musician had to take notice of and reproduce faithfully. For some, the musical score itself had become an object to be valued above anything else. By the end of the twentieth century, many composers had sought to replace the musician themselves and communicate with their audience directly through tape, and later, digital recordings of their music which, to a larger extent, were under their own control through specially prepared recordings or other mechanical reproductive technologies.

The element of control that a composer can exert on a musical performer through a musical score is only part of the story though. All composers expect musicians to play within a particular style that is suitable for their music. Vivaldi would have expected his musicians to provide embellishments to his score (perhaps by adding particular musical effects at key moments to enhance the beauty of a particular melody); Brahms would have frowned on his musicians playing his music in this way and conductors of his music today would also not allow musicians to improvise in this way. By contrast, in many operatic styles the Da Capo aria became the vehicle by which singers were able to show off their vocal virtuosity. Here, the basic structure of the aria (song) contained two main sections – part one and part two. Following the performance of part one and part two, the first part would be repeated but it would be quite wrong for the singer to perform it in the same way as earlier in the aria. The singer was expected to take the basic ideas of the song (the melody) and transform it through their virtuosity into something significantly different. In other words, they had to reinterpret the emotions and feelings within part one in light of the new ideas contained within part two. As opera shifted from a private to a public form of entertainment in the early nineteenth century, audiences would pay vast sums of money to hear specific singers (virtuosi) interpret these Da Capo arias in this way. This resulted in many composers, and others, complaining that the overall narrative of the opera was being hi-jacked (or at least put on one side for the duration of the aria) by the singer for their own personal fame and notoriety.

As with the actor and the world of the theatre, there are some interesting comparisons here to the work of teachers in planning and delivering a lesson. First, as with the previous example, teachers are in that dual position of composing the lesson plan (the score) and delivering it (through their performance); they have a joint role of composer and musician. Our exploration of the role of the score in musical performance raises questions about the amount of detail that may or may not be necessary in the lesson plan and the extent to which any individual teacher needs to be held accountable to the lesson plan as an integral part of their performance. As a young teacher, you may decide to include a lot of information in your early lesson plans. This may help you feel confident during the lesson and give you a series of signals or signposts to help you along the way. But, over time, you may be able to manage with less detail, perhaps just writing down the general structure within the plan itself and allowing space for its embellishment through your pedagogical performance.

The metaphor also allows us to explore the interesting element of audience (student) expectation here. To what extent should the lesson plan and the activities therein build on the 'legitimate' sense of student expectation within lessons? Like the Da Capo aria, the endless repeating of familiar ideas needs to be avoided so the skilful embellishments and extemporisation that a teacher can bring to existing subject content is something that can provide endless challenge for the most experienced of teachers. No two performances of a Da Capo aria should be the same; similarly, no two lessons taught to any group of students will ever be the same (even if they have the same or very similar lesson plans underpinning them). Do you remember question 7 in Chapter 1? My students often ask me whether or not they can use the same lesson plan for similar lessons. My answer is always no! Whilst certain elements may be similar, the group of students you are teaching in any one given lesson are a unique group. They should not be treated the same despite their similarities.

Additionally, the stylistic differences between different types of music have some relevance here too. There are differences in subject approaches to lesson planning and delivery that you will need to bear in mind. For those of you training to be primary school teachers, you may find these differences overwhelming on occasions. This is because they reflect more than just technical differences, but go right to the heart of what individual subjects really are and what they try to achieve as part of a student's formal education. Lesson planning should not look or feel the same for every subject.

For those of you working in the secondary school context, it is important to look beyond your subject boundaries regularly. You will find that there are significant benefits to your own pedagogy as a geography teacher if you spend some time looking at how the drama teacher encourages his students to find their individual voices; as a music teacher you will find significant benefits in looking at how the science teacher organises and curates the various resources needed for a complex experiment. This kind of pedagogical cross-curricularity is something I have noticed on many occasions when I have visited schools around the northwest of England. Perhaps the most interesting example that relates most closely to our discussion of the work of actors and musicians is drawn from the work of one drama teacher I saw teaching a Year 8 class (Savage 2012). In the lesson I saw the teacher make an explicit link to a pedagogical device drawn from the world of the theatre, her 'home' subject. This device was then applied for a new purpose within the classroom. Whilst this might not be considered 'cross-curricular' in the traditional sense, it does reveal an approach to teaching a subject that builds upon its wider heritage and the tools or processes within it.

The specific technique used throughout a significant portion of the lesson was called 'freeze framing'. During the lesson, and as part of a unit of work on developing a character's identity, students were improvising a scene that depicted Rosa Parks' refusal to give up her seat on a bus for a white passenger in Montgomery, Alabama. At key moments, the teacher would shout 'Freeze!' and the students were required to stop what they were doing and remain absolutely still and quiet. At this key moment, they are asked to reflect, in character, about their feelings at that specific moment. In the drama teacher's words:

> I find it a very helpful way to try to understand whether or not the pupil really understands the role of their character. I make use of a technique called 'freeze framing'. This is when the action in a particular scene is frozen at a particular point in time. Normally I will decide when this happens, although sometimes I will let pupils decide. At the particular moment when I shout 'Freeze!', every pupil involved in the scene has to stop what they are doing or saying and remain absolutely still. They stop moving, talking or anything else. This allows us to think together about the situation that the pupils are presenting through their acting. It is a technique drawn from the theatre and it allows a particular actor to talk about their perceptions in the situation they find themselves in or to give the audience further information about how they might be feeling or thinking. Some directors called this 'thought tracking'.
> (Ibid., p. 85)

In interview, I asked the teacher why she had adopted this tool. Again, in her words:

> As a teacher, I use this technique quite a lot to help my understanding of whether pupils are really engaging with a particular scene. I would say it is a key part of my assessment for learning strategy. During the freeze frame moment I will ask questions to a particular character in the scene. Sometimes I will also ask pupils who are watching the scene with me to ask questions too. I find it a very helpful way to try to understand whether or not the pupil is really understands the role of their character. Obviously it has limitations. In drama, pupils often feel things that they can't express in words. But, when used with other assessment devices, freeze framing is a really useful assessment tool. And I'm pleased that it is an adaptation of a tool from the theatre.
> (Ibid., p. 85)

For those of us who are not drama teachers, we could ask ourselves an obvious question: what would 'freeze framing' look like in our subject area?

Teaching as coaching

The final part of our metaphorical journey of the 'performance of teaching' brings me on to the work of footballers. Whilst you might characterise footballers as sportsmen or sportswomen, for the sake of our discussion here let's call them performers! I have chosen to focus on their work for a number of reasons. First, there are a number of similarities with the work of actors and musicians – they work in a group, they are highly skilful as individuals, and they provide a 'performance'. But in contrast to the vast majority of actors and musicians, footballers do not have a script or a score to work towards. Or do they?

A couple of years ago, there was a significant change in the management of the England football team. It caused a lot of press speculation. Whilst the press and many pundits initially favoured the appointment of Harry Redknapp to the position, the appointment of Roy Hodgson in May 2012 came as a surprise to some. One of the concerns that was raised at the time related to the coaching style that Hodgson was purported to favour (Zonal Marking 2012). Whilst working at various clubs around Europe, some professional footballers had found his coaching style too heavy-handed and laborious, involving them walking through particular team movements in what was seen as a stifling way. Pundits jumped on this observation and contrasted it with the work of other football managers who, it was claimed, allowed their players a platform to exhibit their own flair and creativity. In summary, Harry Redknapp, some claimed, was 'all about individuals'; Hodgson, in contrast, was 'the ultimate system manager' (ibid.).

The consequences of these approaches to coaching and team management can be seen by any keen football supporter. Sitting towards the back of a football ground, it is possible to observe the 'shape' of the football team ebbing and flowing as they move between defensive and attacking positions. The eleven players, whilst each being highly skilful and tactically aware as an individual, should be playing as part of a larger team that has to be flexible enough to accommodate and rebut the advances of the other team whilst maximising their own potential to attack and score when the right moment arises.

A metaphorical reflection on the style of coaching that footballers receive gets to the heart of the relationship between lesson planning and lesson delivery. Taken to an extreme, the 'certain anarchy' (ibid.) style of management represented by the work of Redknapp and others could result in a pedagogical style that is all about a teacher's individual flair, exhibitionism and personal charisma. To these teachers, perhaps, the requirement for careful, systematic planning for learning that covers all eventualities (akin to the system management approach of Hodgson) is an anathema. They need to thrive on the freedom and flexibility of their individual talents and not feel encumbered by pedagogical rules or regulations. But for others, a planning approach that covers every square inch of the field, and every eventuality, is seen as preferable. Within that clear structure, these coaches would argue, the individual flair of specific players can be nurtured and developed. For teachers following this model, very detailed planning might be seen as a requirement for teaching that will facilitate every student's learning to their full potential.

But unlike actors and musicians, the footballer metaphor has one unique element that has a massive impact – another team to compete against! The opposition are coached and drilled to exploit your own team and your individual player's weaknesses, and are there to beat you within the rules of the game. Here, I am not conceptualising your students as the opposing team! Rather, I would like to suggest that they do provide the challenge to any teacher's planning and pedagogy. Your challenge is to match your own personal strengths, flair and your planning to the development of a pedagogy that captures and inspires their imagination, making them enthusiastic about their learning and keen to participate fully in your classes. They will also provide that 'grit' against which your teaching will be honed.

In my job I am often asked what makes the perfect teaching placement. Some students imagine that the independent schools, with their small classes and beautifully behaved children, would be perfect for them! Well, first of all, I am not sure that this is always the case. But, more importantly, very well-behaved, passive classes are often the hardest to teach well. A lively group of pupils who respond to your lesson (in good or bad ways) will often give you that immediate feedback that you need as a young teacher to change tack, provide additional support or add more challenge. The perfect teaching placement is one where students are challenging but where you have good mentor support to be able to cope with that challenge and, over time, develop your own individual pedagogy to meet those challenges on your own.

Planning and pedagogy

Metaphorical application and reflection can really help us think differently about the processes of teaching and the development of an effective pedagogy. These performance metaphors raise a number of key points for consideration of how to develop links between planning and pedagogy.

First, all performance activities do require preparation and planning of some sort. In acting, music and football being well prepared with technical skills, stylistic awareness, communication skills and a good sense of teamwork are all necessary criteria for success. These things do not happen by accident. They require dedication over many years, regular practice, analysis and a constant focus on reflection and evaluation of one's own practice. Whilst actors and musicians often work with a script or score, and this imposes certain restrictions on them, even footballers are working within a particular 'system' that may constrain the opportunities for any one player's individual action. In all cases, having a framework for artistic or sporting action is essential to the success of the activity. For us as teachers, the dedication that we need to work on our own pedagogical approach must be undertaken with the same degree of seriousness and long-term commitment.

Second, in all these metaphors there is a tension between the script, the score and the coaching strategy which all seek to impose on the work of the performer, and the desire of the creative actor, musician or footballer who wants to bring their own sense of personality and vision to their work. This could be interpreted as a desire to conform or liberate. Perhaps the moments that an audience most value are when an actor, musician or footballer is able to take that step out of conformity and bring something that is unique and of the moment to that particular audience? However, that process of liberation can be taken too far. We would not want our Shakespearian actors to deviate from the script into some kind of free-flowing narrative; nor would we expect a right-back with defensive duties to abandon his team mates and adopt a careless forward role within a football game. For young teachers, sticking with your lesson plan is a vital first step towards creating this link between planning and pedagogy. You have to lay the groundwork for a more liberated approach to teaching in the conformity of the lesson plan. There is no short cut. Whatever the strengths of your own individual teaching ability, they will need to be honed and developed through the three-staged process of planning, teaching and reflection.

Third, even with the most highly improvisatory forms of theatre, music and team management, there are mental frameworks and schemata within which performers work. This is important. Musical improvisation, when musicians apparently make music up on the spot (combining composition and performance together in the moment), is, essentially, an illusion. Improvisatory musicians have a framework of musical ideas in their minds, generated through hours of practice and pre-rehearsal; improvising jazz musicians have highly developed stylistic languages to draw on, developed through their listening to recordings, so playing one type of chord for Ella Fitzgerald might be highly appropriate whilst for Billie Holiday it would transgress her style. For teachers, apparently making up lessons on the spot should be avoided but experienced teachers will often talk about their best lessons coming to them in an instance, perhaps whilst doing something else completely different. These moments do not appear out of nothing. There will have been a systematic exploration of that particular field of subject teaching and pedagogy that underpins that creative moment. Creativity in lesson planning can happen, but it happens against the backdrop of hard work and effort (in my experience, 99% perspiration and 1% inspiration).

Summary

Jo Salter was one of the first female jet pilots in England. Her account of learning to fly a military jet is fascinating reading and illustrates the variety of teaching and learning methods that are employed to train a top fighter jet pilot. Of particular interest was her account of how you can learn to fly without actually being airborne at all!

> I used to walk around, rehearsing the checks, the switch positions, the radio calls
> – running circuits in my bedroom, plotting air defence tactics across a field,
> circling dogfights on bikes, even flying formation in my sleep. Rehearsal builds
> muscles in the brain and the brain remembers this much more effectively when
> flying and operating an aircraft. It is the beginning of an automated sequence
> where pilots react without thinking – essential for rapid decision-making at life-
> threatening moments. (Salter 2005)

When Salter left the Royal Air Force, she retrained as a teacher. As part of this process, she began to compare the process of learning to fly to the challenges associated with teaching:

> As a teacher I employ the same lessons that I learnt as a student; I rehearse and
> visualise – how I am going to stand and how I am going to use my body language
> in order to convey my message. The spoken word is only part of how we teach.
> We have all experienced the flat teacher, the one who seems to no longer be
> there, whose energy has disappeared and whose presence is blurred. These are
> not the lessons you remember. (Ibid.)

Much of this chapter has been devoted to forging explicit and metaphorical links between planning and pedagogy. To these two Ps, I would like to add a third – practice. Practice is essential in turning your carefully prepared lesson planning into an exciting and stimulating series of opportunities for learning for your students. But practice need not only be done in front of your students. You can practise being a teacher all on your own! Salter's pre-rehearsal strategies and visualisation exercises find and explore common ground in the work of actors, musicians, artists and many sports too. There are numerous ways that you can turn your lesson plan into a living enactment of your lesson and pre-lesson rehearsals are a vital part of turning a lesson plan into a reality. So, why not try:

- Reading through, acting out or practising certain key parts of a lesson plan in privacy.
- Structuring explanatory dialogue or key questions and, if necessary, mentally scripting parts of the lesson plan ensuring that there is clarity and purpose in your words. These can be rehearsed in front of the mirror.
- Imagining responses to various different scenarios and planning courses of action. These need not be extreme situations. It may be something as simple as a pupil

asking an awkward or seemingly irrelevant question. Having a number of good diversion or re-focusing statements up your sleeve can smooth over potentially problematic exchanges.

- Rehearsing a few jokes! There is a significant amount of literature that emphasises the importance of humour in creating positive learning and teaching environments (Garner 2005; Hill 1988). Whilst we may not all be natural wits, there is plenty of time to rehearse and practise a few relevant jokes to insert with your lesson plan. Pupils will really enjoy this element if it is done well.

In closing this chapter, I would like to return to the work of Professor Robin Alexander. In his classic book on pedagogy (Alexander 2008), he describes Douglas Brown, an inspirational and exceptional teacher of English (and much more besides) at the Perse School in Cambridge during the 1950s. Perhaps not surprisingly, the teaching of Brown that Alexander describes throughout his chapter is very different from that which many teachers provide today. For example, Alexander reflects on the way that Brown talked to his classes (p. 156). Apparently he talked a lot! Today, we would criticise him for talking too much as a teacher. Not for Alexander. Douglas Brown's talk was captivating and engaging. Alexander also explores Brown's intellectual, moral and pedagogical approaches which resulted, he says, in a display of the 'humility of genius and the artistry of teaching' at their best. The broad pedagogical approach Brown adopted led Alexander to describe him as not one teacher but four (language, literature, music and the man through whom the power of these was unlocked).

For me, perhaps the most notable thing about Alexander's recollections of Douglas Brown is his description of him as 'not one teacher but four', rather than 'not one teacher but three'. What was the difference? Brown's sense of personality and identity informed his teaching in powerful ways. The greatest subject that Brown taught was life itself. Within his English classes, individual subjects were subsumed through a skilful educational dialogue between teacher and pupil that we would be wise to try to recapture in our schools today.

Within this chapter we have explored the links between lesson planning and pedagogy through the adoption of various metaphors (teaching as science and teaching as performance). We have considered the work of other performers in significant detail and drawn inferences from their work to help our understanding of the links between lesson planning and the classroom where our planning comes to life. In doing so, it is easy to forget that your human character and personality is as important to the act of teaching as are the specific skills of lesson planning, explaining a concept or assessing a learning outcome. Never forget the example of Douglas Brown. It is the person that you are which will provide the power to unlock a love of learning in your students that will span their lifetime.

Reflective reading

Pineau, E. (2005) 'Teaching is performance: Reconceptualising a problematic metaphor'. In Alexander, B., Anderson, G. and Gallegos, B. (eds) *Performance Theories in Education: Power, Pedagogy and the Politics of Identity*. Mahwah, NJ, and London: Lawrence Erlbaum Associates.

This reading explores the two metaphors that I have introduced above in significantly more detail: the teacher as actor and the teacher as artist. Pineau is critical of both metaphors that, she argues, can be reductive and lead to an impoverished educational experience for teachers. But she does suggest an alternative way in which both metaphors can be understood. Read the chapter to find out more!

References

Alexander, R. (2008) *Essays on Pedagogy*. London: Routledge.

Bruner, J. (1996) *The Culture of Education*. Cambridge, MA: Harvard University Press.

Gardner, H. (1999) *Intelligence Reframed: Multiple Intelligences for the 21st Century*. New York: Basic Books.

Garner, R. (2005) 'Humor, analogy, and metaphor: H.A.M. it up in teaching'. *Radical Pedagogy*, 6:2. Also online: http://radicalpedagogy.icaap.org/content/issue6_2/garner.html (accessed 14 January 2010).

Hill, D. (1988) *Humor in the Classroom: A Handbook for Teachers*. Springfield, IL: Charles C. Thomas.

Hirst, P. H. (1965) 'Liberal education and the nature of knowledge'. In Archambault, R. D. (ed.) *Philosophical Analysis and Education*. London: Routledge, pp. 113–38.

Phenix, P. H. (1964) *Realms of Meaning: A Philosophy of the Curriculum for General Education*. New York: McGraw-Hill.

Salter, J. (2005) Final word. *Report*, July/August, p. 30. London: Association of Teachers and Lecturers.

Savage, J. (2012) 'Moving beyond subject boundaries: Four case studies of cross-curricular pedagogy in secondary schools'. *International Journal of Educational Research*, 55, 79–88.

Stenhouse, L. (1975) *An Introduction to Curriculum Research and Development*. London: Heinemann Educational.

Wintour, H. (2013) Boris Johnson fails live IQ test. www.theguardian.com/politics/2013/dec/03/boris-johnson-fails-live-iq-test (accessed 6 December 2013).

Wragg, T. (1997) *The Cubic Curriculum*. London: Routledge.

Zonal Marking (2012) England appoint Roy Hodgson. www.zonalmarking.net/2012/05/01/england-appoint-roy-hodgson/ (accessed 3 November 2012).

9 Evaluating your lesson

Introduction

> It is not enough that teachers' work should be studied; they need to study it themselves. (Stenhouse 1975, p. 143)

> Enquiry counts as research to the extent that it is systematic, but even more to the extent that it can claim to be conscientiously self-critical. (Stenhouse 1985, p. 15)

The first six chapters of this book concerned themselves with issues of planning and preparation for a lesson. In the last chapter we explored a range of metaphors to consider how the delivery of a lesson could be considered as a type of 'performance'. Once the 'performance' of the lesson has been accomplished, the evaluation of the lesson needs to be undertaken. This final chapter will draw together the book's main themes and help you develop a constructive approach to lesson evaluation that views the lesson plan itself and the 'performance' of the lesson as two sides of the same coin. Later in the chapter, links will be made between aspects of educational evaluation and the abilities needed to become a reflective practitioner. We will consider the importance of undertaking more systematic evaluations of your teaching, at particular times and for specific purposes, as well as drawing together some wider points about a constructive approach to your continuing professional development.

The word 'evaluate' means to 'ascertain or set the amount or value of'; or, 'to judge or assess the worth of'; other definitions include the word 'appraise'. The key word at the centre of the word 'evaluate' is 'value'. How can you place a 'value' on a lesson you have taught? How do you measure 'value' in the context of a student's learning? How do you measure 'value' when you are considering a whole group of students learning together? Is it even possible to have a shared sense of what 'value' might mean? Does your view of 'value' differ from that of your headteacher, a school governor, or Ofsted inspector?

These are complicated questions, but education, as we have seen throughout this book, is a complex activity. There are no simple answers here. The processes of teaching and learning involve many different discrete, yet interrelated elements, including people (who are complicated enough on their own!), tools, resources, environmental factors and, most important, different ideologies. Watching teaching and learning take place within a classroom or other learning environment is fascinating. Evaluation provides a way for you to understand the activities that go on in your classrooms. Used productively, it is a tool that you can use to investigate your own practice in a systematic and self-critical way. Evaluation involves specific actions and processes. These include looking at things, asking questions, listening to others, describing events and making interpretations. It is a skilful activity that you will need to practise in order to reap the benefits.

This chapter opened with two quotes from Lawrence Stenhouse, Professor of Education at the University of East Anglia during the latter half of the twentieth century. You may remember that I introduced him at the beginning of the previous chapter in relation to his famous phrase that there is 'no curriculum development without teacher development'. Stenhouse was a tremendous advocate for the teacher. Teachers, he said, were any schools' most important asset and needed to be valued appropriately. Stenhouse developed the view that teachers were in the best place to study teaching through processes of educational research. This resulted, over time, in the methodology of action research that Stenhouse used with teachers across East Anglia to help them explore their teaching practice systematically.

This book is not about promoting this, or any other, form of educational research. But I do believe that there are many similarities within action research and evaluation. You are in the best place to analyse your teaching. Adopting an evaluative stance at the end of each lesson will help you develop the skills of evaluation that will lead to a cycle of reflection and improvement in your teaching. This will have the twin benefits of making you a better teacher as well as maintaining and stimulating your interest in teaching during the course of your career; and, of course, your students will benefit too.

Developing your approach to lesson evaluation

Before we turn our attention to the structures and documentation of evaluation, I want to explore two key evaluation activities you can undertake that are complementary to your teaching role. Finding the links between teaching and evaluation will help you manage your time effectively and avoid you being distracted from your key roles in the classroom. It will also make for a better evaluation and assist you in your own development as a teacher. The two activities are observing and communicating.

The importance of effective observation

As a teacher, you will become used to observing your classroom. It is a key aspect of your teaching role. During every lesson you need to make time to take that step backwards from the complexity of classroom interactions to observe what is going on. This will have many benefits. First, of course, it will help you respond and act in a more informed way during the course of the lesson itself. Building in this 'thinking time' through careful observation is a key part of an effective pedagogy but it takes a determined effort on your part. Classrooms are busy places and it is easy to prioritise other activities in the heat of the lesson itself. Try to resist this, and build in at least one opportunity in every lesson plan to take a detailed look at what is going on in your classroom.

But, second, this type of deliberate observation can form a central part of your evaluation strategy. But you need to be careful here too. The very familiarity with the classroom itself can become a barrier to effective observation. You will need to learn to challenge this familiarity in different ways. It is very easy to lull yourself into a false sense of security and end up seeing what you want to see. Therefore, it will be important to find ways to challenge your own observations, particularly if you are conducting this evaluative work within your own teaching. To this end, we will briefly consider a range of conceptual and practical approaches to observation that will help you do this.

Right at the outset, I would suggest that you reject the idea of one 'true' interpretation for the teaching and learning that is going on within your classroom. Rather, there will be numerous explanations of the teaching and learning that occurs that you will need to consider. Some of these may even be in competition with each other and all of them will be framed by the context of time, place, person and objects that we have explored in various ways throughout this book. Teaching and learning are both heavily contextualised, and these contexts are infinitely variable.

So, from the beginning of your evaluative work as a teacher, learn to live with uncertainty in your observations. When you are watching others teaching or your own students' learning, remember that your own thoughts are framed by notions of objectivity and subjectivity which you could spend a lifetime exploring. You do not have time to do that now! Rather, look for examples of activities in your own and your students' work that are 'credible and defensible rather than true' (Kushner 1992a, p. 1). Whilst observing, use your instincts to look out for interesting responses that students make within the lesson, unusual responses in particular activities, or that spark of creativity that a student may show at a given moment. These types of responses offer you an insight into the learning that is being facilitated by the opportunities you have constructed through your lesson planning.

Third, digital technologies can be very helpful observational tools. These tools, whether they record audio or video, can literally put you in a different observational place. The analysis of the recordings that you obtain can reveal interesting points that you may have missed in the busyness of a lesson. The downside of this approach is that it takes a long time to review recorded materials. I would encourage you to be selective about your use of these tools for that reason. But having said that, the benefits can be significant. So, if you want to explore and analyse your own pedagogy, why not consider video recording yourself? Recording yourself as a teacher is no different from those disciplines such as acting, dancing or athletics where video analysis is central to the improvement of performance. It is no different for our work as teachers.

Fourth, be focused in your observations. Remember that your lesson has specific learning objectives and outcomes. As we will see below, the key purpose of your lesson evaluation will be to ascertain whether or not these learning objectives and outcomes have been met within the context of your lesson. Your observations must focus on these and, hopefully, produce the evidence that you need to make key decisions about future planning. But also remember that learning objectives and learning outcomes should not be thought of as being fixed in stone. They will develop as the lesson unfolds and you will need to be responsive to the outworking of these throughout the lesson, documenting their developing through your lesson evaluation.

Finally in this section on the importance of effective observation, get into the habit of making very brief notes as you observe your classroom. This is not the time for extended essay writing! However, key thoughts about what is being observed tend to be fleeting. You need to be able to capture these in your notes. I would suggest that you always have a small notebook to hand to jot down thoughts as they occur. These can be referred to later when you get to the stage of writing up your formal lesson evaluation.

PRACTICAL TASK

Take one or two points from the discussion above and practise them the next time you get an opportunity to observe another teacher working or teach a lesson yourself. Ask yourself, what does it really mean to 'see well'?

The importance of communication

As a general rule, watch students working before you talk to them about what they are doing. I found this to be a particularly useful principle in my work as a secondary school music teacher. In many of my music lessons, students worked together in small groups on a musical performance or composition. Watching, and listening, to them working in these groups was always a source of high-quality evaluative information.

Following observation, good communication with students is central to effective teaching and learning and a very useful evaluative skill. Non-verbal forms of communication such as gesture, body language or facial expression should not be forgotten, but it is your verbal communications with students that will probably be a principal focus in your early lesson evaluations.

Right from the outset of your teaching, try to be natural in your conversations with pupils. Whilst you will have many different 'voices' that you will want to develop to help build your identity in the classroom, you need to reserve a calm, enquiring type of voice for your interactions with individuals or small groups of students. Try to build on your existing relationship with the class, or the individual student, and seek to develop conversations around the key learning objectives of your lesson. But do this in a natural, not a forced, way. Asking the right sort of questions will be an important skill. As we discussed in Chapter 3, scripting questions for use within your teaching episodes is good practice and should form part of your early lesson planning. Some of these questions may well be related to your evaluation activity in a lesson.

Second, listen to the conversations that pupils are having between themselves during the various teaching episodes and the activities contained therein. These often contain really important evidence that can usefully inform your evaluation. As I have mentioned already, observe first and resist the urge to interrupt too soon. When you do initiate a conversation about the activities or the learning objectives that you are trying to promote, do not close down the possibilities of alternative viewpoints that may arise from the students' perspectives.

Finally, allow conversations to touch on elements of your teaching as well as focusing on the students' learning. This can be difficult, and even awkward, for experienced teachers. But it can prove very enlightening. If you are undertaking a teaching placement as part of a programme of initial teacher education, it is highly likely that you will be teaching in a number of different schools during the year. This presents a particularly rich opportunity to obtain a range of student feedback (and you may not be in that school for that long either) so be bold and ask! Take a deep breath and, perhaps, be prepared for one or two difficult conversations. The feedback you receive from students about your teaching can be extremely valuable.

In your lesson evaluations, you will need to reflect on the conversations that you have had with your students. But do not fall into the trap of believing everything that you hear! A legitimate aspect of evaluation is judging or ascertaining the worth of particular pieces of evidence. Sometimes, students are just plain wrong, ill-informed or may just be being mischievous. You will need to take a range of views into account and an essential voice within this mix will be your own. Although recent educational initiatives have given a priority to 'student voice', there have been critics of this approach. For some, the emphasis on student voice is nothing more than adults 'copping out' and an 'abdication of their responsibilities' (Paton 2009). In the same article, a Professor Hayes goes on to say:

> Everywhere I go the clearest sign of the rejection of adult authority is listening to learner, student, pupil [or] infant voice. Anybody's voice but the voice of adults. I love debating with pupils and students and getting them to research but basically they know nothing. ... You are all professionals and you are saying that all you have to do is listen to young people. Well, you are abandoning your jobs – your role as adults – and you will make education in the future impossible. (Ibid.)

Perhaps a balanced view of teacher and curriculum development needs to reassert the role of the teacher as a professional alongside that of the student voice. Within the sphere of lesson evaluation, your voice is as vital as anyone else's voice. So do not underplay what you think and say about your own and your students' work.

By using these simple techniques of observation and communication you will be able to collect a range of evaluation data about your lesson. Data sounds a bit grand, but in practice, as we have seen, it can be quite simple. It will probably include short comments about teaching sessions, notes about your thoughts or feelings during any evaluation processes within the lesson, snapshots of conversations with pupils or other things that come to your mind and might be useful later on.

REFLECTIVE TASK

In what ways can I build a structured approach to the valuing of student voice in my lesson evaluations? Given the one hundred and one things I have to do during a lesson, how can I keep track of comments students make or conversations I have with them for evaluation later on?

Before we turn our attention to the lesson evaluation document itself, remember that the plenary and mini-plenary episodes in your lessons can be an invaluable opportunity to collect this type of data, and that you do not have to do all the work yourself! As we considered in Chapter 5, using a range of assessment for learning techniques including self-evaluation and peer-assessment will not only help you assess your students' work in a convivial way, but will also give you access to a range of evaluative perspectives that observation and communication alone may not facilitate. In my experience, students do not mind you being open about the dual purpose of plenaries, that is, as a vehicle for assessment and evaluation, providing that they are well structured, get to the point and do not require them answering the same questions time and time again. It is better to be up-front with them about this rather than keep evaluation (like assessment) hidden from them.

Constructing your lesson evaluation

Throughout your initial teacher education, and the early part of your teaching career, I would strongly recommend that you complete a lesson evaluation for every lesson that you teach. Whilst some might think that this is a little too prescriptive, I cannot overemphasise the importance of regularly planning, teaching and evaluating lessons. Evaluation is as important a part of that cycle as planning. Never teach a lesson without a lesson plan in the early part of your teaching career; and never miss the opportunity to reflect upon and evaluate your work. It is vital to becoming a skilful and competent teacher.

There are various ways that you can construct your lesson evaluation. As part of a programme of initial teacher education, your tutors may have given you a template; there are many others available online. Like the adoption of a particular lesson plan template, it is not the purpose of this book to force you to adopt a particular lesson evaluation template or document. You will need to consider what format is going to work best for you. But whatever format you do use, there will be several key areas that you want to address.

Evaluate the learning objectives, the learning outcomes and teaching activities

Every lesson that you plan will have learning objectives, learning outcomes and teaching activities housed within episodes. In your lesson evaluation, look back on the learning objectives in light of the lesson you have taught. Were they met? If so, were they challenging enough? If not, were they too far removed from students' current level of understanding? Did all the students meet them? Who did? Who did not? Why not? These, and other questions (see below), will help you chart the progress of your students' learning week by week.

Similarly, what learning outcomes did the students exhibit? Were they what you expected in terms of their relationship to the learning objectives you had set? Were there any surprising learning outcomes that you did not anticipate? Are these worthy of further consideration as you begin to plan your next lesson?

The teaching activities of the lesson are also worthy of careful analysis. Did they provide the best form of engagement for the students? Were they focused enough on the particular learning objectives you were hoping to promote? Were there any practical issues to do with resources, environment, or other factors that influenced the flow of the teaching activities?

These three areas constitute the main building blocks of most lessons that you will teach. However, you will also want to consider other elements of your pedagogy within your lesson evaluation.

Evaluate your own performance

As I have mentioned already, teaching is a skilful activity that, over time, you should improve in. However, this improvement does not occur by accident. It is the result of a deliberate process of planning, practice and reflection. In each phase of your teaching, you will have key areas for improvement (perhaps identified at the start of your teaching placement or via a process of performance management) that you will want to reflect on. Your lesson evaluation is an ideal place to start this process and maintain it through the regular cycle of planning, teaching and evaluation.

So, lesson evaluations can be a good process by which to discuss the nitty-gritty of your teaching. Try to think in detail about specific elements of your pedagogy (e.g. how you questioned a pupil, how you modelled a specific process, how you used a new behaviour management strategy, where you stood in the room, your body language, your tone of voice – the list really is endless!) and discuss it, briefly in your evaluation. And, most importantly, use this opportunity to set yourself another target in that area (for reflection and evaluation later on). At specific moments within this type of evaluative work, you should also consider the main strategies for differentiation, personalisation and assessment that you are including within your planning for specific lessons.

In the early stages of your teaching, you may be working closely with a more experienced colleague who is acting as your mentor. This provides a valuable opportunity to get detailed and focused feedback on your pedagogy. Through discussion, ask for specific focus points and then use your lesson evaluations to reflect on these. On occasions, you may receive more explicit instructions (i.e. you really must improve X or Y). Constructive critical feedback of this type is also invaluable. Use the evaluations that you complete lesson by lesson to show a positive response to this advice and guidance. Done well, they can provoke constructive discussions in your mentor meetings and create a positive impression of your engagement and progress in your mentor's mind.

Evaluate your students' learning

Hopefully, part of this will be covered in your evaluation of the learning objectives, learning outcomes and teaching activities that you have completed in the section above. But here, try to be even more explicit. I would encourage you to reflect on and evaluate the learning made by one or two students specifically (i.e. name them and talk about what they have managed to achieve). It would certainly be appropriate here to talk about strategies of differentiation and personalisation and how they have been applied to particular pupils (perhaps those with SEN or those on the gifted and talented register). Over time, if you adopt this strategy, you will build on some detailed portraits of individual students and their learning. This can prove invaluable when it comes to reporting back to parents about the progress of their child in your class.

Think ahead

Finally, use your lesson evaluation form to build a bridge into your planning for the next lesson with the class. Throughout this book, I have urged you to consider this three-part, cyclical process of planning, teaching and evaluating. Your lesson evaluation for one lesson really must complete this cycle and result in informed decisions for your next lesson.

Done in this way, lesson evaluations become part of a meaningful strategy of pedagogical improvement, not just a chore to complete. I will emphasise this again. There are no short cuts here. The best route to a long and fulfilled career as a teacher is to plan, teach and evaluate in a cyclical process.

Like many professions, teachers have a very busy professional life. There will be many competing and varied demands on your time. You will need to learn to be an effective time manager, to prioritise and deal effectively with students, parents and other colleagues. But this three-staged process is, for me, of central importance in learning to become an outstanding teacher. Clearly, you will make your own decisions here. But ignore this advice at your peril!

Extending evaluation to medium- and longer-term planning

These approaches to lesson evaluation can be usefully extended into other areas of your work. One obvious application would be in helping you consider the medium- and longer-term planning that your individual lesson planning is situated within. As we saw in Chapter 7, the exact structures that you might use will vary depending on whether or not you are working in a primary or secondary school, but the general principles apply equally. Medium- and longer-term planning contain many similar elements to your individual lesson plans. You will need to consider the impact of these plans in the same way, although perhaps not with the same degree of frequency, as your individual lesson plans. Periodically, you may decide to evaluate:

- The construction of a specific unit of work within a particular year of study, e.g. the Year 9 unit of work on calculus.

- The impact of a whole key stage programme within a particular subject area, e.g. my Key Stage 2 programme of study for History.

- The different ways that teachers within your school or department teach a particular topic, e.g. approaches to the teaching of long division within the team of Mathematics teachers.

- A specific element of teaching within a chosen subject area, e.g. how to teach perspective in Art to Key Stage 2 students.

- Something else of your own choosing!

Although this broader process of evaluation should be considered as a separate activity from the lesson-by-lesson evaluation of your own teaching and your students' learning, clearly there are going to be links that you can draw. Having decided to evaluate a particular set of medium- or longer-term plans, I would immediately undertake a review of your own lesson evaluations that relate to that particular part of your curriculum – perhaps completed in previous years. In doing so, you will be looking for helpful insights into the construction of the medium- or longer-term plan rather than the detailed comments about specific elements of a lesson. Once completed, you may have a number of key reflective points that you can build into a more focused, longer-term evaluation of the unit of work. If information is lacking at this point, do not worry. You can now plan for the opportunity to conduct a more detailed evaluation in your chosen area.

Establishing the evaluation focus and sharing your design

Although your time to devote to an evaluation of this type may be limited, particularly in the early days of your career or if you are working on your own, it is always worth trying to define the wider context of your proposed evaluation. This could involve a number of different activities. First of all, ask yourself whether similar pieces of evaluation have been undertaken elsewhere? If you have not got the time to do significant searching of written or electronic sources, posting a short question on a teacher website/forum (such as the *Times Educational Supplement*) may be worthwhile. Local authority advisers can often have a helpful overview of work that is going on in different schools. Universities with education departments may also be a helpful point of contact. Seeking out comparative studies or undertaking analysis of related documents is not going to provide the evaluative answers that you are searching for. These will only come as you study your own work in a systematic way. But they will provide potential sources of illumination for you, or, to use a contrasting metaphor, they will provide hooks onto which you can hang your own evaluative thinking.

Through these discussions, reading and analysis you can helpfully establish and refine a focus for your own evaluation. You will want to make sure that this is something that is achievable and manageable within the context you have chosen. There is no point in setting yourself up to fail. I think it is important not to rush at this point. Deciding to undertake a focused evaluation study on an area of your work can be a substantial undertaking. Please make sure that the focus area, or question, that you are wanting to consider through the evaluation is worthy of the time and energy that you will have to put in to it.

This leads on to the second key point. Sharing your thoughts about your evaluation study at an early stage is important. Who might you share this with? In the context of a piece of curriculum evaluation, I would urge you to share your ideas with the senior manager within your school who has a responsibility for the curriculum at the appropriate key stage or subject area. Whilst this might have an effect on the political dimension of your work (i.e. you probably do not want to upset your senior managers!), as you are working within a management system where accountability is important and they probably have a right to know what is going on. But, more important than that, by sharing your ideas at this early stage you are showing yourself to be a reflective practitioner, someone who is wanting to initiate change in their teaching in a systematic and responsible way. You may also want to share your thinking about the proposed evaluation in other forums too. It is helpful to get feedback from a group of colleagues whose judgements you trust and with whom you can share ideas without fear of ridicule or rejection.

Conducting your evaluation

You have decided on a focus for your evaluation. You have searched around for similar studies, shared your ideas with your senior manager and other selected colleagues, and reflected on their advice. You are ready to go. What are you going to actually do during the evaluation itself? What are the activities that you can undertake, alongside your teaching, to help collect the data that you need to understand more fully the impact of a particular aspect of your medium- or longer-term planning?

First, the activities of observation and communication that I described above are going to be just as relevant to this evaluation as they will be for your lesson evaluations. Learning to see well, and communicate well, are vital skills. Clearly, the focus points for your observations of, and communication with, students are going to be different. You may be concerned about the sequencing and development of learning across a broader time span than an individual lesson; you may be interested in considering how their learning pathways develop around key concepts or critical incidents that have been planned for across the key stage; you may be comparing and contrasting the pedagogies of individual teachers and seeking to develop a notion of what might be considered best practice in a particular area. For all these reasons, and doubtless many more that you can think of for yourself, your observations and communications with students and other teachers may take on a different dimension with an evaluation study like this.

There is one further activity that I have found to be very useful in evaluative studies of this sort that I would like to add to our discussion at this point: interviewing. Interviewing has a long history in educational research and it can prove to be a very beneficial approach within evaluations too. There are many guides on how to conduct interviews with young people either within educational research (Kvale 2007) or as part of a clinical setting (Ginsburg 1997). There are a number of important points to consider here.

First, all interviews are structured by the values and intentions of the interviewer. Although different writers may emphasise the importance of open-ended or semi-structured interviews, I would suggest that it is not worth getting too hung up on concepts like this for too long. Within the context of talking to your students, or perhaps to other staff, it will be more important to consider whether or not your interview is going to be about information-retrieval or whether it will be more developmental in its nature.

Interviews that are about information-retrieval make a number of assumptions. They assume that the interviewee(s) (in our case, the student, students, or perhaps a teaching colleague) knows something that the interviewer (you!) does not know. The task of the interview is to extract that information. The skills that you need in this context will be about putting the interviewee(s) at ease, asking appropriate questions and facilitating the resulting conversation in a way that exposes the information that you deem, or think, is important. This is a perfectly legitimate approach to interviewing and one that, given the limited time that you have for an evaluation of this sort, may be the approach to adopt first.

However, there is a second way that interviews can be conducted that may be even more beneficial. The 'developmental interview' is underpinned by a different range of assumptions. As Kushner explains:

> This approach assumes that the interviewee probably does not know either and the task of the interviewer is to set up a learning situation. The interviewee is seen as someone locked up in a role and unable to take an objective role of what he or she knows, so the task of the interview is to prise the person out of the role and to ask them to look back at it and evaluate it. The interview is typified by exploration, by asking many supplementary questions to clarify and extend an idea. ... The focus is on the individual rather than the project – their life and values. The idea is to see the project in the context of the person's life. (Kushner 1992b, p. 1)

This approach to interviewing is more time-consuming. But, as Kushner points out in a later point in his exposition, it can be conducted over a longer period of time, perhaps as an interview that takes place on a number of separate occasions or stages. For you as a teacher, this type of dialogue with a student could be constructed over the duration of a unit of work, or even a whole key stage. By asking the right sort of questions, students could also engage with this type of focus through written responses as well as in a face-to-face interview situation. This may also be less threatening from their perspective.

This moves us on to a final point about interviewing. If you are going to include interviewing in your evaluation (and I would encourage you to do so), try to make them a sense of occasion from the students' perspective. In my own evaluation work as a teacher, I would often try to find opportunities outside the formal time of a lesson to talk to students about their work. I used to regularly conduct lunchtime 'interviews', where pupils could relax, eat their lunches and talk about their work on a particular project. I found that this was more relaxing for me too. I have also found that group interviews are often better in this respect. Students can bounce their ideas off each other and, when this is going well, you can often find yourself taking a back seat in the interview process completely. In my experience, this is a good sign that the interview is moving beyond the 'information-retrieval' approach and really entering a developmental phase.

In the evaluation phases, you will be utilising a range of methods or processes to collect data that relates to the specific focus of your evaluation. In the best evaluations, this data comes from a range of sources including, but not limited to, documentary analysis, comparative studies, observations, informal communications and interviews.

Reaching judgements about your work

You have reached the end of the designated evaluation period. You have observed students working, you have talked to them about their work, you have done a range of interviews and discussed your evaluation as it has unfolded with other colleagues. In a parallel stream of activity, as part of your day-to-day teaching, you have assessed your students' work within that unit of work using a range of formative and summative assessment techniques. Your assessment data is collated and organised efficiently and you have been able to provide top-level data to your senior manager. You are faced with a collection of evidence in various formats drawn from your assessment and evaluative processes. It is time to reach some judgements about your work.

One of the key ways of making judgements from a piece of evaluation work of this type is to ask yourself questions about the data you have collected. Perhaps this is easier when you are working collaboratively, but the kind of internal questioning that is essential to reflective practice is also a vital activity at this stage of the evaluation process. In no particular order, these are the types of questions that will make a good starting point:

- What are the consequences of the evaluation on myself, my students and my colleagues?

- How does the data in my evaluation relate to other changes that I am being asked to make?

- Where do the values come from that underpin this evaluation? Are they from my experiences or beliefs, or are they from somewhere else?

- Who have been the winners and losers in this piece of evaluation?

- How would you describe the teaching approaches observed within the evaluation period? Has it been authoritarian or democratic, formal or informal? What aspects of my own or others' pedagogy have changed or developed from a traditional, subject-based pedagogy?

- How have the students learnt in this unit? In what ways have they learnt differently than they might have done in a more traditional approach to the same topic? What have you learnt by the whole experience?

- Were my original aims, objectives and activities for the evaluation appropriate? How did they change and develop over the duration of the project?

- If I had to do the evaluation again, what would I change?

- Whose knowledge really counts within an evaluation like this?

- How could the collaborative dimensions and evaluation be translated into an individual teacher's pedagogical approach?

■ Are there any conflicting pieces of evidence within the evaluation? Is it possible to reconcile these in any way?

Although I am suggesting these questions as a good starting point, they may or may not all be appropriate for the piece of evaluation work that you have undertaken. I would encourage you to view this as an important stage in the evaluative process. Learning to ask the right questions about your work is a crucial part of the process of reaching a judgement within your evaluation.

This process of questioning can continue for some time. Pragmatically, you are going to have to draw a line under your evaluation at a particular point and move forwards. So reaching a conclusion, in your mind or as a written report of the evaluation, is an important final step. I would encourage you to write up the evaluation, however briefly, as an integral part of this process. I opened this chapter with a couple of quotations from the great Professor of Education, Lawrence Stenhouse. For him, educational research and curriculum development (of which I would count this kind of evaluative activity) was 'systematic enquiry made public' (Stenhouse 1975). The 'making public' part of this definition is crucial, partly because it provides a system of accountability but, more importantly, making your findings public will help create a dialogue of ideas about teaching and learning that will benefit you and others. Within your context of your work as a teacher in a primary or secondary school, 'making public' the findings of your evaluation might mean sharing them at a staff meeting, or writing a report for a senior manager. But it might also mean sharing them within a subject association, or at education conference, or a Teach Meet, or within an online forum.

As an example of this type of approach, at a meeting of the governing body on which I used to serve, we received an article, via the headteacher's termly report, from a teacher of Mathematics working at the school. Her evaluation had looked at the process of implementing a more explicit assessment for learning approach within her teaching of Mathematics. The report was a scholarly account of her approach, characterised by the constructive use of data drawn from many of the processes of observation, communication and interview that we have discussed throughout this chapter. The student voice was evident within her study, but also her own professional opinions shone through, backed up with evidence drawn from various sources. Having completed the study, this teacher was asked to present her work and associated findings to the rest of the staff within the school. Her approach had been adopted and adapted to help provide a broader assessment for learning strategy within the school as a whole. Through various external links that the school had, she was invited to attend a meeting of local authority advisory staff and present her work to them. This was well received and further studies were commissioned.

This type of evaluation empowers the individual teacher. Unlike the cycle of planning, teaching and evaluation that should underpin your daily work, this more extended evaluation process is not going to be an everyday occurrence. But when done well, it has many longer-term benefits for your work as a teacher. In a political era of top-down educational initiatives that can often overwhelm teachers and result in them feeling like they are constantly having to play 'catch up', it reasserts your own authority and places you at the centre of the process of curriculum development. It does take time (and this may put some teachers off), but I would encourage you to do it on occasions. It is time that is richly rewarding for you and your students.

Conclusion: commit to becoming a reflective teacher

As this book reaches its closing pages, it is time to offer some concluding thoughts. Lesson planning, of the type described within this book, is a truly creative and challenging activity. Closely allied to the development of one's pedagogy as a teacher and the principles of evaluation that we have explored in this chapter, it is part of a cyclical process that can sustain a long and productive career in teaching.

As I have been writing this book, I have found myself reflecting on my own work as a teacher, my experiences of watching young teachers teaching, the programmes of initial teacher education that I am responsible for working within, and also on some of the key literature that I have read over many years. Writers such as Elliot Eisner, Saville Kushner, Lawrence Stenhouse and others have been a constant source of inspiration and challenge to my own teaching, thinking and writing.

Whatever the implications are of my distance from the immediate work of teachers, I hope you have found this book a helpful one in considering the processes of learning to plan high-quality lessons and teach them well. In concluding this book, I would like to turn to a common notion that I feel is helpful for us all in our work: the reflective teacher.

My thesaurus has the following entry for 'reflection': 'a calm, lengthy, intent consideration'; it follows this with words such as 'musing, rumination, thoughtfulness, contemplation, reflexion, meditation, introspection and speculation'. So, what does it mean to be a reflective teacher? Drawing on the work of Donald Schön (Schön 1983, pp. 332–4), I think it involves the following. The reflective teacher:

- Listens to their students and really seeks to understand them as unique individuals, tailoring their instruction, speech and learning resources to respond to their specific requirements.

- Thinks beyond their lesson plan in seeking to respond to individual students' needs and requirements.

- Uses the curriculum as an inventory of themes to be understood rather than a set of materials to be learnt.

- Expands their knowledge of the students to encompass their learning and interests outside of the classroom.

- Uses technology in a way to empower students to undertake their own learning rather than to reinforce old-fashioned, teacher-centric pedagogies.

- Prioritises independent, qualitative, narrative accounts of learning over blunt, accountability-driven assessment frameworks that depersonalise the student and their achievements.

- Challenges set theories of knowledge and its organisation within the school systems of timetables and classrooms, seeking to make links in imaginative ways across and in between subject boundaries.

But, you might argue, surely the general busyness of school life can compromise any well-meaning approach to aspire to become a reflective teacher? This is a danger. But Schön and other writers on reflective practice recognise this and, more importantly, identify the larger structural forces at work in any school that can compromise an individual's attempt to be reflective. Schön asks us to imagine a school whose work is characterised by a range of features (some of which you may recognise). It is:

- Built around a theory of knowledge which dictates that it is the teachers' job to teach and students to learn. Knowledge is imparted by teachers in 'measurable doses', with students digesting these chunks and teachers planning for students' progressive development.

- Orderly, in terms of space and time. It has self-contained classrooms and a regular timetable through which knowledge bases (subjects) are partitioned and delivered.

- Controlled by systems of sanctions and rewards for students, with expectations for individual students set and checked regularly.

- Controlled by systems of sanction and rewards for staff, with management structures ensuring standards are maintained.

- Characterised by objectivity, with quantitative measures of proficiency and progress preferred to qualitative or narrative accounts of learning and teaching.

This bureaucratic model of schooling imposes significant restraints on the work of the aspiring reflective teacher. However, Schön says, it need not quash it completely. Part of working through a process of reflective practice is seeking to develop an understanding of forces that can mitigate against it.

So, how can you develop the art of being a reflective teacher? First, make a firm commitment to practise the art of being a reflective teacher. This is a very important psychological first step. Second, find a short period of time each day, even if it is just a few minutes, to reflect on the teaching you have engaged with during the day. Ask yourself simple questions such as:

- What went well?

- What did not go so well?

▨ How could you improve things?

▨ What would you do differently next time?

Next, keep a teaching journal. This might not be something that you choose to do all the time. But, on occasions and for specific reasons (perhaps during a period of evaluation), keep a teaching journal by your side throughout your teaching day and jot notes in there for consideration once the physical act of teaching your lessons is complete. Reading your notes, and jotting down your responses in a journal like this will become an addictive and fascinating reflective activity; but do not let it become your master. It does not matter if you have a day off!

Finally, if possible, find a colleague to help share your reflections and act as a 'critical friend'. I remember my first job at Stowmarket High School in Suffolk. I was one of about seven or eight newly qualified teachers each given a Year 9 form to tutor. It was a great experience because it was one that we could share together at key moments throughout the year.

I would argue that reflection is an essential type of activity for all teachers to undertake regardless of their age, experience or position. Reflective practice can start simply and quietly, in your own mind or in a private teaching journal. It need not be part of a grand scale process of performance management or other form of accountability. It is too important to be compromised by them. Why not make that commitment to become a reflective teacher today? It will be the best decision that you can make for your future teaching career.

However you respond to this advice, I hope that you have found this book a useful introduction to the principles and processes of lesson planning and pedagogy. I would like to wish every reader of this book a long and happy teaching career.

Further reading

McIntosh, P. (2010) *Action Research and Reflective Practice*. London: Routledge.

In this book McIntosh examines the relationship between action research and reflection in considerable detail. His notions of 'thinking in action' and 'thinking on action' are particularly informative for the practice of evaluating lessons or other sequences of learning.

References

Ginsburg, H. P. (1997) *Entering the Child's Mind: The Clinical Interview in Psychological Research and Practice.* Cambridge: Cambridge University Press.

Kushner, S. (1992a) *The Arts, Education and Evaluation: An Introductory Pack with Practical Exercises.* 'Section 5: Making observations'. Norwich: Centre for Applied Research in Education, University of East Anglia.

Kushner, S. (1992b) *The Arts, Education and Evaluation: An Introductory Pack with Practical Exercises*. 'Section 6: Interviewing'. Norwich: Centre for Applied Research in Education, University of East Anglia

Kvale, S. (2007) *Doing Interviews*. London: Sage.

Paton, G. (2009) Adults 'abdicating responsibility' for children. www.telegraph.co.uk/education/6598138/Adults-abdicating-responsibility-for-children.html (accessed 10 December 2013).

Schön, D. (1983) *The Reflective Practitioner: How Professionals Think in Action*. New York: Basic Books.

Stenhouse, L. (1985) *Research as a Basis for Teaching*. London: Heinemann Educational Books.

Stenhouse, L. (1975) *An Introduction to Curriculum Research and Development*. London: Heinemann Educational.

Index